KILLER ROCKS FROM OUTER SPACE

KILLER ROCKS FROM OUTER SPACE

ASTEROIDS, COMETS, AND METEORITES

STEVEN N. KOPPES

LERNER PUBLICATIONS COMPANY • MINNEAPOLIS

To my mother, Mary, and my late father, Ralph, who both instilled in me a love of reading and writing.

The author wishes to express his debt to the late Dr. Robert S. Dietz for introducing him to the field of catastrophic impact geology and for the many fascinating hours of interviews he granted the author before his death in 1995. Also to Dr. Dietz's longtime collaborator, Dr. John McHone, for sharing his expertise and for reviewing an early draft of several chapters of this book. Likewise to Dr. Mark Boslough of Sandia National Laboratories. Further thanks go to Conrad J. Storad, who encouraged the author to propose this book to Lerner Publications Company, and to editor Joelle Riley for her insightful suggestions and deft editing.

The publisher wishes to thank Dr. David Morrison, Director of Space, NASA Ames Research Center, for his assistance in the preparation of this book.

Lerner Publications Company
A division of Lerner Publishing Group
241 First Avenue North
Minneapolis, MN 55401

Website address: www.lernerbooks.com

Library of Congress Cataloging-in-Publication Data

Koppes, Steven N.
   Killer rocks from outer space : asteroids, comets, and meteorites / by Steven N. Koppes.
      p.   cm. — (Discovery!)
   Summary: Describes the role that collisions with meteors, comets, and asteroids have played in the history of Earth and other planets in the solar system and examines what is being done to protect Earth from future collisions. Includes index.
    ISBN: 0–8225–2861–4 (lib. bdg. : alk. paper)
    1. Asteroids—Juvenile literature. 2. Comets—Juvenile literature. 3. Meteorites—Juvenile literature. [1. Asteroids. 2. Comets. 3. Meteorites.] I. Title. II. Discovery! (Lerner Publications Company)
   QB651.K58 2004
   523.5—dc21   2003010077

Manufactured in the United States of America
1 2 3 4 5 6 – DP – 09 08 07 06 05 04

CONTENTS

INTRODUCTION

On July 15, 1994, twenty-one large lumps of dusty ice silently streaked through outer space at 134,000 miles an hour. Known as comet Shoemaker-Levy 9, or simply SL9, the lumps were leftover debris from the birth of the Sun and planets. They would soon come to an abrupt end after a journey of 4.5 billion years.

At their solid nucleus, or core, comets consist of ice, dust, and rock. Their orbits take them far beyond the orbits of Neptune and Pluto, the most distant planets in the solar system. As a comet approaches the Sun, the ice in its frozen nucleus turns into gas, giving the comet a halo and a long tail.

Astronomers had known for months that comet SL9 would crash into Jupiter, the largest planet in the solar system. For the first time in history, humans would witness what before they could only imagine: the collision between a comet and a planet. The power unleashed by a nuclear blast was puny in comparison. The former Soviet Union detonated a 58-megaton hydrogen bomb in 1961. It was the largest bomb ever. All told, comet SL9 packed as much energy upon impact as thousands upon thousands of 58-megaton bombs. The debris produced by the explosions vaporized as it fell through Jupiter's atmosphere, generating huge bursts of infrared (heat) radiation.

Jupiter consists mostly of hydrogen, helium, and other gases. Some observers, therefore, had cautiously predicted that they would see no signs of the impact on the planet. But a few

(Left) Comet Shoemaker-Levy 9 strikes the surface of Jupiter, our solar system's largest planet.

groups of scientists expected to see a good show. Teams of scientists at the National Aeronautics and Space Administration's Ames Research Center in Mountain View, California, and at Sandia National Laboratories in Albuquerque, New Mexico, used powerful computers to predict the results of the impact. They calculated that if the largest chunks of the comet were at least 0.6 mile wide, the collisions would become visible from Earth soon after impact.

Those computer simulations proved quite accurate. The vaporizing impact debris produced temperatures as high as 13,000 degrees Fahrenheit, even hotter than the Sun's surface. The impacts and their aftermath looked especially bright through infrared telescopes, which detect heat instead of light. Before it was over, even people with small backyard telescopes could see large, dark spots that the impact had left on Jupiter.

No one on Earth saw the comet's long chain of fragments hit Jupiter's backside. But Jupiter rotates completely once every ten hours, so the impact sites soon came into view. Scientists made observations from instruments in space as well as from observatories around the world.

The comet had been discovered in March 1993 by Eugene Shoemaker of the U.S. Geological Survey in Flagstaff, Arizona; his wife, comet hunter Carolyn Shoemaker; and their scientific partner, astronomer David Levy of Tucson, Arizona. They quickly recognized it as a fragmented comet. One astronomer later called it "a string of pearls." The string consisted of twenty-one fragments spread over 2.5 million miles, more than ten times the average distance between Earth and the Moon.

Jupiter's gravity had pulled the comet apart. This probably happened when the comet passed near Jupiter on July 7, 1992.

SL9 was torn into twenty-one pieces by Jupiter's gravitational pull.

On that date, the comet's orbit took it within 16,000 miles of the gas giant, just a hair's breadth in astronomical terms.

The sizes of the comet's fragments have never been precisely determined. The best estimates indicate that the largest fragment may have measured more than 2 miles in diameter. The comet's very first fragment produced an impressive fireball, and that piece was one of the smallest. The fireball towered 2,000 miles high and spread 4,000 miles wide. The dark spot that formed in Jupiter's atmosphere at the first impact site reached a size half as wide as Earth. The seventh fragment measured possibly 2.5 miles in diameter before its crash. It was among several that produced enough heat upon impact to briefly outshine the entire planet when viewed by telescopes that detect infrared radiation.

The destruction of SL9's largest fragments ended on July 24. Once the bulk of the comet was gone, about twenty large, black bruises remained in the atmosphere of Jupiter's southern hemisphere. Smaller pieces of SL9 continued to plow into Jupiter for another two months.

Scientists learned a lot about cosmic collisions from SL9, but so did society in general. People who usually ignored science took notice. So did Congress, which asked the National Aeronautics and Space Administration (NASA) for a proposal to map and track all large comets and asteroids in orbits that might threaten Earth. Asteroids are rocks that ordinarily orbit the Sun in a belt between the orbits of Mars and Jupiter. But sometimes collisions between the asteroids or the pull of Jupiter's gravity can hurl them into Earth's path. Most comets and asteroids present no danger. If large enough, though, both comets and asteroids can do serious damage to any planet that gets in their way.

Small pieces of comets or asteroids regularly break off and enter Earth's atmosphere. We see them streaking across the night sky as meteors. Most meteors are no larger than sand grains. They burn up quickly in the atmosphere. The ones that are large enough to reach the ground are called meteorites. Most can be traced back to the asteroids.

Comet SL9 left marks on Jupiter's atmosphere the size of Earth. A band of impact debris remained a year after the impact. If a comet or asteroid the size of SL9 hit Earth, it would destroy civilization. The odds are against any large cosmic objects smacking into Earth anytime soon. Still, it has happened many times before, and it will happen again. The only question is when. It might not happen for a million years. It might happen tomorrow.

Fortunately, astronomers—scientists who study objects in the sky—have begun a systematic search for comets and asteroids that might be on a collision course with Earth. Other scientists have studied the results of such cosmic impacts.

Geologists, experts in the formation and destruction of rocks, have investigated craters that catastrophic impacts left behind on Earth, the Moon, Mars, and other planets. Paleontologists, scientists who specialize in fossils, have discovered how an asteroid impact helped to destroy the dinosaurs sixty-five million years ago. Still other experts have learned how impacts may have made it possible for life to spring forth on Earth to begin with. And space probes have visited or will visit a variety of comets and asteroids to learn more about these potentially dangerous objects.

The story of cosmic impact shows how science progresses over the course of decades and even centuries. Science is, above all else, an exciting process, not just a dry collection of unchanging facts.

Chapter 1

RECOGNIZING METEORITES AND IMPACT CRATERS

You can think of Meteor Crater in Arizona as a giant bullet hole. Reaching a depth of 570 feet, the crater could swallow the Washington Monument. Fifteen football games could be played on the floor of this super bowl at the same time. A ring of 4,200 people could stand shoulder to shoulder to watch the games from the crater rim, which measures 1.2 miles in diameter.

The bullet that made the crater was a nickel-iron asteroid approximately 100 feet in diameter. It shot through space at about 45,000 miles an hour. An object moving that fast could travel from Earth to the Moon in less than six hours. It takes a spacecraft four days to make the same trip.

This cosmic bullet would have torn through Earth's atmosphere with a thunderous roar. Burning brightly, it would have seemed as if a piece of the Sun had broken away and come crashing to Earth.

Fortunately, no humans lived in Arizona when Meteor Crater was formed. The impact explosion released as much energy as a medium-sized nuclear bomb. The blast generated hurricane-force winds that would have been felt at least 12 miles away. More than 300 million tons of rock were thrown out of the crater. An awesome mushroom cloud towered into the sky.

(Left) Arizona's Meteor Crater

Fifty thousand years later, scientists accept the impact origin of Meteor Crater as a well-established fact. But they used to think otherwise. For well into the twentieth century, most experts considered Meteor Crater to be an extinct volcano. Who could blame them? Little more than two hundred years ago, the idea that even small rocks could fall from the sky seemed ridiculous. By 1900 it had become obvious that meteorites did come from above. But certainly they were too small and too slow to leave huge holes behind.

● ROCKS FROM THE SKY?

Not until the late eighteenth century did careful observation and experimentation become the primary tools of science. Before that time, scholars often mixed their scientific beliefs with superstition and folklore. Pliny the Elder, who lived in ancient Rome nearly two thousand years ago, believed that rocks could fall from the sky. But he thought that fossils, flesh, blood, bricks, and other unlikely objects could, too.

Earth's earliest recorded meteorite falls were preserved for religious, not scientific, reasons. A 1-pound meteorite fell in Japan on May 19, A.D. 861. It became a treasured relic of a Shinto shrine in Nogata-shi. Likewise, a 279-pound meteorite that tore through the skies over Germany on November 7, 1492, ended up in a church in Ensisheim.

Scholars of the Middle Ages often repeated Pliny's errors. Scientists of the late eighteenth century were more skeptical. Still, at first they failed to take meteorites seriously, even when witnesses had seen them fall. Then came the German scientist Ernst F. F. Chladni. He became a founder of meteoritics, the science of meteorites.

Unlike other scientists, Chladni believed the eyewitness accounts of meteorite falls. To him the stories rang true because reports from different places and times sounded much the same. More importantly, he realized that meteors were falling rocks from outer space. (This idea had earlier been recognized by the English astronomer Edmond Halley, who discovered the famous Halley's comet.) In 1794 Chladni published a book in which he said that meteorites also come from space. At first, most of Chladni's fellow scientists ignored his book.

By 1800 members of the French Royal Academy, a group of highly respected scholars, had studied the chemicals contained in two meteorites. The French scientists mistakenly concluded that both rocks had come from Earth rather than from space.

A study conducted at about the same time in London produced different results. English chemist Edward Howard and a French mineralogist, the Comte de Bournon, examined four meteorites. They determined that the meteorites seemed similar to one another but different from Earth rocks. Howard and de Bournon considered the possibility that meteorites came from meteors, but they stopped short of saying so conclusively.

Other European scientists soon chimed in with studies of their own that confirmed the unearthly composition of meteorites. Some scientists suggested that the rocks formed in volcanoes, either on Earth or on the Moon. Still other experts thought that meteorites somehow could have formed in Earth's atmosphere.

As if on cue, two thousand meteorites showered the L'Aigle area in northern France at 1:00 P.M. on April 26, 1803. The French scientist Jean-Baptiste Biot carefully studied the event. He talked to witnesses and examined meteorites that remained at the scene. His report helped show that meteorites were worthy of scientific study. Finally, other experts agreed with Chladni that meteorites came from space.

Even the largest meteorites then known were too small to pose any serious threat to Earth. Comets and asteroids were something else.

● LEXELL'S COMET VISITS EARTH

Edmond Halley had begun charting the orbits of comets in the late seventeenth century. He noticed that sometimes they crossed Earth's orbit. Halley recognized that some of these objects could potentially hit Earth.

For centuries, superstitious folk had thought of comets as omens of calamity and suffering. Many people living in Britain in Halley's time still did. Author Jonathan Swift made fun of

This medieval German manuscript illustration shows how comets have been feared as bad omens for centuries.

these ideas in his famous book, *Gulliver's Travels.* Swift's book described the people of the make-believe island of Laputa. The people of Laputa lived in fear that a comet's impact would set off a chain of events ending in Earth's destruction.

Halley died in 1742, so he missed Earth's closest known encounter with a comet. That occurred on July 1, 1770, when scientists observed the close approach of Lexell's comet. According to their computations, the comet passed within approximately 1.4 million miles of Earth—about six times the distance between Earth and the Moon. That may seem like a great distance. In the infinite wilderness of the stars, however, it counts as a relatively close shave.

The existence of asteroids remained unknown to science for three more decades. An Italian astronomer was first to discover one, Ceres, on January 1, 1801. A German astronomer discovered Pallas in 1802 and Vesta in 1804. These are the largest of about one million rocky bodies in the asteroid belt.

A SLOW START FOR IMPACT SCIENCE

When objects from outer space hit a rocky planet such as Earth at high speed, they leave behind impact craters. Even so, the study of impact craters developed separately from the study of meteorites, comets, and asteroids.

The great Italian astronomer Galileo Galilei published a study of the Moon's craters in 1610. He could tell that craters were bowl-shaped structures from the way sunlight swept across the landscape, shining first on the raised crater rims, then on their floors. He did not try to explain how the craters formed.

Educated guesses about what caused lunar cratering finally arose in 1665. Edward Hooke conducted some simple experiments that would help him understand both impact craters and volcanoes. Hooke dropped round objects into wet clay to simulate impact. He boiled gypsum, a white mineral used to make plaster, as a model for volcanism (volcanic activity). His impact experiments produced craters more like those he observed on the Moon than his gypsum experiments did. Yet he wrongly decided that

Moon History

Impact and volcanism on the Moon are as tangled as the arms of two wrestling octopuses. Geologists untie the knots by studying lunar rock samples and analyzing data from space probes. Unlike Earth's surface, the dry, airless surface of the Moon preserves impact craters extremely well.

The Moon formed about 4.5 billion years ago. In the earliest phase of lunar history, impacts were large and frequent, generating enough heat to keep the Moon's surface soft and molten. Over time, the surface solidified. Then, more than 4 billion years ago, the oldest lunar impact basins formed: Nectaris, Humorum, and Crisum. About 3 to 4 billion years ago, the Imbrium and Orientale impact basins formed. This was a time of massive lava flows. Lava filled some of the impact basins, producing the lunar maria. These vast, dark areas cover nearly one-fifth of the Moon's surface.

About 1 to 3 billion years ago came some additional volcanic activity and the formation of impact craters such as Eratosthenes. These craters are young enough that geologists have been able to link them with secondary craters. (Secondary craters are created by blocks of material thrown out from primary craters.) Craters formed during this period are too old, however, to have crater rays. These bright streaks of impact debris radiate from young craters like the spokes of a bicycle wheel. Marking the final phase of lunar history, beginning about 1 billion years ago, are the formation of Copernicus and other large craters that still show bright crater rays. Some lava may also have seeped onto the surface during this period.

lunar craters were volcanic. In those days, everyone thought space was empty. Where would the missiles come from?

The study of lunar impact fared no better a century later. An English astronomer claimed to have witnessed three volcanic eruptions in the shadow of the new Moon on April 19, 1787, and another the following day. This would have been impossible. While the Moon once had active volcanoes that produced vast lava flows, they had been dead for billions of years. Still, the claim led some French scientists in the early 1800s to wonder if the Moon could be the source of Earth's meteorites. Some volcanoes produce volcanic bombs, blobs of lava that harden after being expelled violently into the air. Could the Moon's volcanoes have launched volcanic bombs toward Earth?

Lunar impact had one believer in 1829, but his opinion didn't count for much. In 1822 this man had reported seeing people, animals, and the ruins of a city on the Moon!

In 1837 two German astronomers wrote a book that set impact science back a century. The book argued in convincing detail that volcanoes produced the Moon's craters. As a result, most astronomers turned their attention to other matters.

METEOR CRATER ATTRACTS ATTENTION

The study of volcanoes fell squarely into the young field of geology, which had only begun to take shape by 1800. Geologists agreed with astronomers that the Moon's craters were volcanic. They favored that theory because their studies had shown them that changes in Earth's landscape take place slowly.

Modern geologists call this idea of slow change *uniformitarianism*. Simply stated, it means that geological processes such as erosion that are happening in the present are the key to understanding the past. These processes take millions of years to change the landscape. But a meteorite crater forms in an instant. That was too fast for the uniformitarians.

Some early geologists did recognize that Earth sometimes undergoes quick, massive changes. Geologists call this idea *catastrophism*. The influential French scholar Georges Cuvier was a geologist. He believed that the day-to-day forces of nature alone could not explain some of his observations. Cuvier noticed that types of fossils found in one layer of rock were often not present in the next, where different fossils appeared. He explained the changes by proposing a series of four great floods. He said the floods had wiped out old species to make way for new ones.

GEORGES CUVIER

Geology needs both ideas. Sometimes geologic change happens rapidly, sometimes slowly. But during the nineteenth century, the catastrophists lost the argument to the uniformitarians. As a result, geologists overlooked meteorite impacts as important events in Earth's history.

In the late nineteenth century, Grove K. Gilbert of the U.S. Geological Survey did set foot, at least temporarily, on the path toward cosmic impact. Gilbert visited Arizona's Meteor Crater, then called Coon Butte, in 1891. The next year he wrote an insightful report on the impact origin of the Moon's craters. But he came to the wrong conclusion about Meteor Crater. Despite his suspicions that it might have been caused by impact, he proposed that Meteor Crater was volcanic because he found evidence of volcanic activity in the area.

The Geologic Record

Earth began its 4.5-billion-year history as a ball of molten rock. The rock eventually cooled and hardened. Over thousands and millions of years, forces such as wind and water eroded (wore away) particles of the rock. These particles, as well as the remains of dead plants and animals, formed layers of sediments (material deposited by water). The layers thickened as eroded particles continued to accumulate. Eventually the weight of the deposits compressed them into sedimentary rock. Beds of sand, for example, became layers of sandstone. If conditions were right, the buried remains of plants and animals were preserved as fossils.

After centuries of careful study, geologists have learned to read these sedimentary rock layers like the pages of a book. Each rock layer corresponds to a page in Earth's history. Some pages, or even entire chapters, are missing. Some were eroded away. Perhaps conditions kept others from forming in the first place.

Chemists can assign ages to many of these rock layers by analyzing the chemical elements that are present. Geologists can then use the ages of rock layers to help determine the age of a meteorite impact scar (the eroded remains of an older crater). If an impact scar sits on top of undisturbed sediments that are seventy-five million years old, then the impact scar has to be less than seventy-five million years old. If the scar is buried under sediments that are twenty-five million years old, on the other hand, then the impact scar has to be more than twenty-five million years old.

This reasoning comes from two basic principles of geology. The principle of crosscutting states that a geologic feature such as an impact scar must be younger than the rock layers it cuts through. The principle of superposition, meanwhile, states that except under special circumstances (such as the overturning of rock layers by an earthquake), younger layers of rock always sit on top of older layers.

Geologist and mining engineer Daniel M. Barringer of Philadelphia, Pennsylvania, set scientific thinking about Meteor Crater back on course. In 1902 Barringer learned about the crater and the countless nickel-iron meteorites found nearby. He and a scientist friend, Benjamin C. Tilghman, quickly became convinced of the crater's meteoric birth, sight unseen.

DANIEL M. BARRINGER

Barringer and Tilghman believed that the mass that had created Meteor Crater lay buried underneath it. Gilbert had thought so, too, at first. But a large, buried mass of nickel and iron would deflect a compass needle away from magnetic north. Gilbert detected no unusual magnetic readings in the area. Barringer and Tilghman had an answer for that: the meteorite had broken apart upon impact, thereby escaping Gilbert's detection.

Expecting to find a fortune in minerals, Barringer and Tilghman formed the Standard Mining Company and staked their claims. But the meteorite had not simply broken apart. It had mostly vaporized in the impact explosion. Tilghman dropped out of the company in 1909, several thousand dollars poorer.

The crater must have seemed like a bottomless pit to Barringer. His company spent $6 million at the crater over a twenty-five-year period. He drilled as deep as 1,376 feet, but came up empty-handed. Barringer nonetheless produced a scientific gold mine at Meteor Crater that continues to yield nuggets of knowledge.

Both he and Tilghman published scientific papers arguing that impact caused the crater. These papers enlisted a few scientists behind their theory, but only a few. Barringer kept looking for evidence until his death in 1929. By that time, scientists had begun to accept the crater's impact origin.

During the 1930s, evidence for meteorite impact began to pour in from craters all over the world. It came from Africa, Australia, and Arabia, as well as from Argentina in South America and Estonia in northeastern Europe. In the United States, even Kansas could boast of its own crater near tiny Haviland.

After decades of controversy, the impact origin of Meteor Crater was accepted by 1959. A few diehards still clung to volcanism to explain the origin of impact scars. But Eugene Shoemaker's studies in northeastern Arizona helped establish some important differences between impact and volcanic features.

In his work for the U.S. Geological Survey, Shoemaker found volcanic vents (openings through which lava erupts) under maar craters, which are craters caused by volcanic explosions. The rims of maar craters contain thin layers of volcanic ash. Beneath Meteor Crater is pulverized rock. The crater's rim is a collar of overturned rock, with no volcanic ash. The rim of the Teapot Ess crater in Nevada has similar overturned rock along its rim. This is significant because the Teapot Ess crater was produced by a 1.2-kiloton underground explosion, not a volcanic eruption.

Present-day scientists recognize Meteor Crater as the best example of an impact crater on Earth. Still, it is easy to see why geologists were slow to recognize the crater for what it was. The surrounding region contained extensive evidence of volcanism. It was simply bad luck for scientists that the meteorite landed where it did.

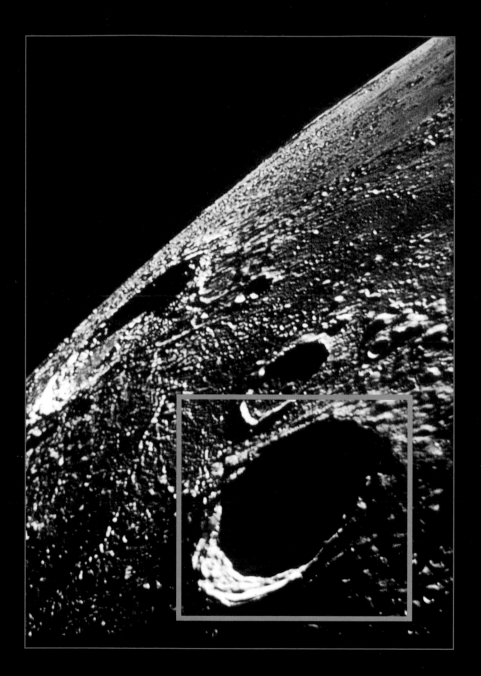

Chapter 2

IDENTIFYING IMPACT SCARS

Cosmic bombs have blasted tens of thousands of craters into the face of the Moon during the past several billion years. Surely Earth has also been a target. But where are all the craters? In fact, scientists know of about 170 impact craters and heavily eroded impact scars on Earth. The list grows longer every year.

The best-preserved impact crater is Meteor Crater. Most impact scars are far older and far less obvious. Scientists call these scars *astroblemes,* which is Greek for "star wounds." Astroblemes are old craters that have mostly disappeared due to erosion and other forces of nature. Geologists can identify eroded craters by the subtle clues they leave behind, both on the surface and below the ground.

Lunar craters survive virtually forever because the Moon is a dead planet. It has no blowing wind, flowing water, or crust (surface) movement to hide or destroy its craters. The situation on Earth is quite different. One geologist has estimated that all traces of a crater measuring 12 miles in diameter could disappear completely from Earth's surface in 120 million years. That is why half of all known craters on Earth are less than 200 million years old, although Earth is 4.5 billion years old. Meteor Crater

(Left) The Moon's crater Copernicus is a well-preserved impact scar.

is only 50,000 years old. After another few hundred million years, it, too, will be difficult to recognize as an impact scar.

Scientists have found astroblemes all over the world—hidden in the jungles of South America, partially buried in the desert sands of Africa, and even submerged beneath the waters of the Atlantic Ocean. In Canada, one astrobleme actually sits partially atop a much older, larger astrobleme.

◉ SHATTER CONES PROVIDE A CLUE

Sometimes astroblemes are found by accident. But Robert S. Dietz found a way to look for them. In the late 1940s, Dietz began to suspect that shatter cones could be used to prove that a geologic structure was an impact scar. Shatter cones are cone-shaped, wrinkled-looking rocks that are caused by the shock of meteorite impact. They range in size from about 0.5 inch to 40 feet long. They can occur in any kind of rock, but they form especially well in limestone. Shatter cones are usually found near the center of large impact structures. The number of sites with shatter cones has climbed to more than sixty—nearly half the world's proven or suspected impact structures.

The pressure produced by an impact is measured in units called atmospheres. The pressure exerted at sea level by the weight of a column of air extending to the top of Earth's atmosphere is 1 atmosphere. Water is heavier than air, so the pressure in the ocean at a depth of only 33 feet is 2 atmospheres. The deepest point in the ocean is the Marianas Trench in the Pacific, which is 35,839 feet deep. At the bottom of the Marianas Trench, the pressure is about 1,090 atmospheres. Impact pressures, by comparison, range from a bit under 2,000 to more than 100,000 atmospheres. Shatter cones formed

Shatter cones have been found all over the world. These were discovered in southwestern Montana.

under relatively low impact pressures of 2,000 to 10,000 atmospheres.

The scientific world had first learned of shatter cones in 1905. Two German scientists had discovered shatter cones at the Steinheim Basin in Germany, but they failed to recognize them as a fingerprint of meteorite impact. Instead, they thought the Steinheim Basin was the result of a muffled (underground) volcanic explosion. They called such explosions "cryptovolcanic." The word *crypto* is Greek for "hidden."

Dietz had first encountered shatter cones at a rock quarry near Kentland, Indiana. The idea that the shatter cones were part of an impact scar did not immediately occur to him. The Kentland structure was several hundred million years old. Its crater, once measuring 8 miles in diameter, had long since eroded away. But geologists still examined its shatter cones. They also puzzled over its rock layers—a central area of jumbled, overturned layers was surrounded by normal, flat-lying layers. A careful field inspection of the Kentland shatter cones revealed that they all had originally pointed toward the same spot above the ground. This suggested that a force from above, rather than below, had made them.

By the late 1950s, shatter cones had been found in Tennessee and Missouri as well as in Indiana and Germany. All four locations had the jumbled rock layers that most scientists of the time regarded as signs of muffled volcanism. But if intense volcanic shock produced shatter cones, why hadn't they been found near any of Earth's hundreds of active volcanoes? Shatter cones and messy, circular jumbles of rock hinted at meteorite impact. But scientists needed more evidence to tell the difference between an impact scar and the remains of a volcanic explosion.

Dietz figured that high-speed meteorite impacts generated shock waves much more intense than those produced by volcanism. In his opinion, a high-speed meteorite impact left behind shatter cones as surely as a careless thief leaves fingerprints at the scene of a crime.

Eugene Shoemaker suspected the same thing. Early in his career, Shoemaker had accepted the muffled volcanism theory. But once he understood just how violent volcanic eruptions are, he realized that the cryptovolcanism theory made no sense. There is no such thing as a muffled volcanic eruption. If an explosion takes place within a volcano, the pressure is released through the volcano's throat—it does not stay under the ground.

Shoemaker and engineer Donald Gault were able to produce small shatter cones in the laboratory in 1960. Gault worked at the NASA Ames Research Center near San Francisco. He was using a gas gun to test how much damage tiny meteorites would cause if they hit a spacecraft. Shoemaker and Gault used the gas gun to make shatter cones by firing aluminum pellets at 3.4 miles per second into a limestone target.

Just a few years later, investigations turned up shatter cones at what would become the world's two oldest and largest known impact structures. The Vredefort structure in South Africa measures 186 miles in diameter and is approximately 2 billion years old. The Sudbury structure in Ontario, Canada, measures 155 miles in diameter and is about 1.8 billion years old.

Only a few geologists in the late 1930s and early 1940s suspected that Vredefort was an impact structure. South African geologists recognized that Vredefort was unusual. Still, they used unlikely theories involving specific combinations of earth movements and lava flows to explain how it had formed.

Dietz became interested in Vredefort in the early 1960s. He had gone looking for an Earth crater similar to the lunar crater

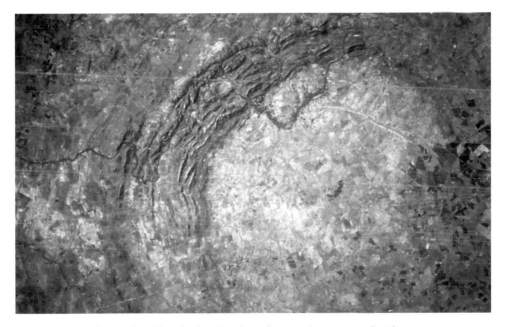

South Africa's Vredefort structure is one of the largest and oldest impact scars on Earth.

Copernicus. Copernicus is one of the Moon's largest, at 58 miles in diameter. Dietz wondered if shatter cones existed at Vredefort. He couldn't visit to see for himself, so he asked South African geologist Robert Hargraves to look for him. Hargraves easily found shatter cones on his first visit. At first, the theory that Vredefort had been caused by meteorite impact was controversial among geologists familiar with the region. The same would be true of Sudbury.

Sudbury was famous for its complex geology as well as its rich ores, which were discovered in 1883 and still provide much of the world's nickel. Dietz became interested in Sudbury while looking for features on Earth similar to lunar maria—the vast, dark, lava-filled areas of the Moon. At Sudbury, an upwelling of magma (molten rock from within Earth) had broken the surface and cooled into a broad, nearly flat dish of lava. Atop the lava sat a 1-mile-thick layer of rock that resembled hardened volcanic ash.

Acting on a hunch, Dietz conducted a brief field inspection of Sudbury. He had predicted that he would find shatter cones, and he did. But he also observed other evidence of impact. For example, he noticed that the overturned rock layers at the southern end of the structure resembled those at Meteor Crater.

In 1964 Dietz published a paper presenting his impact theory of the origin of the Sudbury structure. The paper shocked Canadian geologists. They had already identified ten likely meteorite-impact sites in their country, ranging from 1.2 miles in diameter at Holleford, Ontario, to 39 miles in diameter at Manicouagan, Quebec. But Sudbury had escaped their attention.

Dietz's theory that a nickel-iron meteorite had bombed Sudbury was difficult for the geologists of the time to accept. But present-day geologists generally agree on the complex sequence of events that unfolded there approximately 1.8 billion years ago. At that time, the region was a quiet coastal area on a young Earth mostly populated by simple plants like fungi and algae. Suddenly, a meteorite several miles wide struck the area. As Dietz once put it, Sudbury's rock layers sprang up somewhat like a flower opening its petals on a sunny day. Some of the layers were completely overturned.

The intense heat and pressure of impact melted the rock where the meteorite hit into a large pool of lava that partially filled the crater. Debris thrown into the air by the impact rained back into the crater, forming a 1-mile-thick layer over the lava pool. The lava slowly cooled to form a top, lighter layer of granite and a bottom, heavier layer of basalt. Over time, water and minerals eroded from the crater walls covered the lava pool. One billion years later, movements in Earth's crust created a mountain range to the southeast of Sudbury, pressing the originally round basin into its current oval shape.

THE DISCOVERY OF ANCIENT SCARS

In 1967, shatter cones called attention to a previously unnoticed old, large impact structure by the St. Lawrence River about 60 miles northeast of Quebec in Canada. It was the first time that shatter cones had led to the discovery of an impact structure.

Called Charlevoix, the structure measures approximately 33 miles in diameter. Like Sudbury, Charlevoix had escaped notice by Canadian geologists and the aerial photographic search for impact craters conducted by the Dominion Observatory of Canada.

Charlevoix's great age no doubt helped conceal its existence. Only its central peak—a feature seen only in very large impact structures—and a semicircular valley remain of the original crater. Once scientists found shatter cones at Charlevoix, they

Charlevoix was overlooked as an impact scar until shatter cones were discovered there.

noticed other telltale signs of impact. Various forms of melted, deformed, and shocked rock were present.

Shatter cones also led to Robert Hargraves's discovery of the Beaverhead, Montana, site in 1989. Beaverhead was another ancient impact. The ages of the rock layers in which shatter cones have been found show that the impact took place between 345 million and 1.3 billion years ago. Little remains of the original structure. The glaciers (large, slow-moving masses of ice) and other geologic upheaval of the last several hundred million years have erased most traces. But the crater may originally have measured more than 35 miles across.

● THE TRANSFORMATION OF QUARTZ

Meteorite impact leaves other traces besides shatter cones. Scientists have found that the pressure of impact damages quartz in special ways. Quartz is a mineral commonly found in sand. Just as pure carbon turns into diamond under high pressure, quartz turns into minerals called stishovite and coesite.

Stishovite forms when quartz is subjected to impact pressures of 12,000 to 15,000 atmospheres. Coesite forms under pressures of more than 30,000 atmospheres. Both minerals were produced in laboratory experiments—coesite in 1953, stishovite in 1961—before they were found in nature.

Eugene Shoemaker and his colleague Ed Chao found coesite scattered throughout a layer of sandstone in Meteor Crater in 1960. It was unlikely that any natural force other than impact had enough power to produce coesite. Therefore any location at which it was found would almost certainly have to be an impact structure. Sure enough, scientists quickly discovered coesite at four more sites around the world. Three were impact sites and one was a nuclear test site. Chao and three other scientists soon found stishovite at Meteor Crater, too.

Shoemaker and Chao had opened up a new scientific field: shock metamorphism. This new field focused on the ways that rock changes when subjected to the intense forces of impact.

Besides stishovite and coesite, another type of shock metamorphism is shocked quartz. This type of impact damage forms under pressures of approximately 10,000 to 20,000 atmospheres. When examined under a microscope, the damaged quartz looks like it has a series of parallel slats.

⦿ TEKTITES: FROM EARTH OR THE MOON?

Impact can melt rock as well as shock it. When rock is melted by impact, objects called tektites are produced. These objects have baffled scientists for more than 160 years.

Tektites are lumps of black, green, or yellowish-brown glass. They come in teardrops, dumbells, and other odd, fluid shapes. The smallest tektites are microscopic. The largest weigh more than 7 pounds. Sometimes they can be traced back to the crater where they were formed, and sometimes they can't. The areas in which tektites are found are called strewnfields.

Charles Darwin, the nineteenth-century scientist who developed the theory of evolution, found tektites on Ascension Island in the South Atlantic while on expedition aboard H.M.S. *Beagle* in 1836. He mistook them for volcanic bombs. At first they fooled even Virgil E. Barnes, the man who later became one of the foremost experts on tektites. Barnes, a geologist at the University of Texas, spent much of his career studying these objects.

In 1940 Barnes thought lightning strikes might have melted rock, causing tektites to form. Later, he decided that they were glass meteorites. After much study and debate, Barnes and his colleagues realized that tektites were rocks that had been melted on impact and violently ejected from the ground. The bits of melted rock had rapidly cooled and resolidified as they flew hundreds or thousands of miles through the air.

Billy Glass, a graduate student in marine (ocean) geology at Columbia University in New York, discovered microtektites in the mid-1960s. He found the tiny glass pellets in samples dredged from the floor of the Indian Ocean by researchers from Columbia's Lamont-Doherty Geological Observatory. Scientists would eventually find oceanic tektites in three of the world's four largest tektite strewnfields.

A few experts remained unswayed by Barnes's meteorite-impact theory of tektite formation. Some preferred to believe that tektites came from lunar volcanoes. Others thought the lumps of glass were the remains of a destroyed planet. But over time, most scientists

Tektites come in a variety of sizes, shapes, and colors,

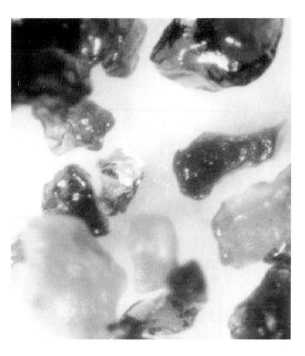

have come to agree with Barnes's theory. Tektites typically contain high concentrations of silica, a common Earth mineral. This implies that they formed on Earth. Also, their odd shapes are what you might expect from rocks formed by catastrophic impact.

Chemically, tektites are different from the rocks and soil they are found among. Clearly, tektites came from somewhere other than where they are found. Based on their composition, the tektites found in Ivory Coast in Africa apparently came from the Bosumtwi crater in Ghana, which formed about 1.3 million years ago. The Ries Basin impact in Germany, which occurred approximately 14.9 million years ago, could have produced central Europe's tektites, known as moldavite tektites. The source for the tektites spread from Texas to Georgia could be the 35-million-year-old Chesapeake Bay crater in Virginia.

But no crater has been connected with the 700,000-year-old Australasian tektites found in Australia and Southeast Asia. The Australasian strewnfield is the largest of the world's four major tektite strewnfields, covering 10 percent of Earth's surface. It is a roughly triangular area that measures about 6,200 miles on each side. The triangle's base stretches from the Indian Ocean east of Madagascar to a point south of eastern Australia, about halfway between Australia and Antarctica. The top of the triangle lies off the coast of Japan.

Three types of Australasian tektites have been found: Muong Nong tektites, teardrops, and australites. Together with the microtektites taken from the seafloor, they would add up to form a sphere about 660 feet in diameter.

The chunky Muong Nong tektites, named for a village in Laos, are found in northern Indonesia. The splashy-looking teardrop forms are mixed in with the Muong Nong type in Indonesia, the Philippines, and Southeast Asia. Australia has the australites, which are flattened spheres that resemble buttons. The shape of the australites shows that they traveled faster and

MAJOR TEKTITE STREWNFIELDS

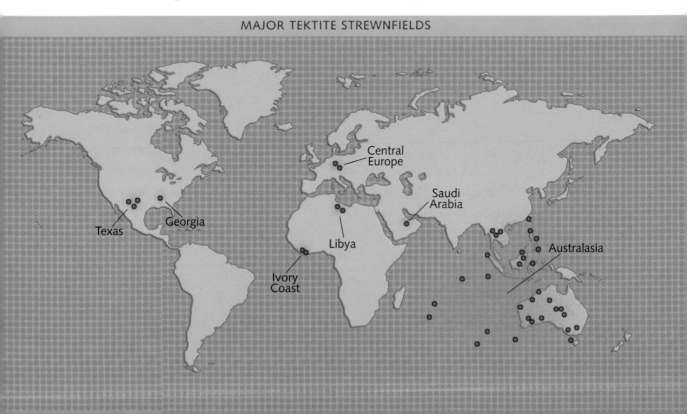

farther than the other two types of tektites. They were partially melted away or vaporized as they blasted through Earth's atmosphere at a speed of 5 miles per second.

The placement of the three types of Australasian tektites suggests that the impact that produced them took place in Southeast Asia, perhaps in Cambodia or Vietnam. The crater from which they were thrown must be big. Major tektite fields are associated only with craters more than 6 miles in diameter. Africa's Bosumtwi crater, which produced the Ivory Coast tektites, is 6.5 miles in diameter. Germany's Ries crater, which produced the moldavite tektites, is 15.5 miles in diameter.

A broad scattering of bits of glass in the Libyan Desert of western Egypt is another strewnfield in search of a crater. The Libyan glasses are scattered over about 4,000 square miles. They are as puzzling today as when they were discovered in 1932. Like tektites, they consist almost entirely of silica. But the glasses lack smooth, aerodynamic shapes. Their irregular shapes suggest that they were not thrown through the air. Still, many researchers consider them to be a special class of tektites.

Two scientists at Vanderbilt University, in Nashville, Tennessee, proposed that the desert glass resulted from a comet's collision with Earth. According to this theory, the Libyan glasses are the hardened remains of sand that was melted by the impact. Some of the molten sand was thrown into the air, but some remained within the crater and hardened to form the Libyan glasses. The impact would have happened about thirty million years ago, leaving a crater up to 4 miles in diameter.

Chapter 3

IMPACT AND THE DINOSAURS

Astronomers estimate that a mountain-sized comet or asteroid crashes into Earth about once every 100 million years. If so, the dinosaurs got off lucky—they lived on Earth for approximately 163 million years. Their luck finally ran out 65 million years ago, at the end of the Cretaceous period.

That is when an asteroid measuring 6 to 10 miles in diameter blasted into the northern coast of the Yucatán Peninsula, in Central America. The impact caused, or at least contributed to, the extinction of the dinosaurs and many other prehistoric life-forms.

For years, paleontologists worked on the mystery of dinosaur extinction. Had massive volcanic activity over a long period of time killed them off? Or was their extinction caused by dramatic changes in sea level or climate? No one knew for sure. Then came evidence that impact might have played a role.

◉ EVIDENCE TURNED TO DUST

A team of scientists at the University of California, Berkeley, came across the evidence quite unexpectedly. Nobel Prize-winning physicist Luis Alvarez, his son, geologist Walter Alvarez, and two chemists were measuring the fall of dust particles from

(**Left**) A paleontologist examines dinosaur tracks in Arizona's Painted Desert.

Luis **(left)** and Walter Alvarez examine a sample of an iridium layer.

space. They were trying to learn how long it had taken for ancient rock layers to be deposited.

Meteoritic dust particles fall to Earth steadily. They contain iridium, a chemical element rare in Earth's crust but common in meteorites. At Gubbio, in northern Italy, the Alvarez team had found a higher-than-normal concentration of iridium in a thin layer of rock deposited at the end of the Cretaceous period, when the dinosaurs went extinct. The team also found late-Cretaceous iridium layers in Denmark and New Zealand.

According to the Alvarez team, the iridium came from a large asteroid that had collided with Earth. The impact explosion hurled a huge dust cloud into the atmosphere, blocking the Sun's light. A long period of global darkness followed. The darkness lowered the temperature of Earth's atmosphere. It also slowed plant growth, leaving plant-eating animals with little food. Death claimed predator and prey alike as food sources dwindled.

The dust cloud, which contained iridium and other traces of the asteroid, settled to Earth about sixty-five million years ago. Its minerals formed a distinct layer between those deposited in the

Cretaceous and Tertiary periods. This iridium-rich layer is called the K-T boundary. (The *K* stands for *Kreide*, a German word meaning "chalk." *Cretaceous* itself comes from *creta*, which is Latin for "chalk." Many chalk deposits formed during the Cretaceous.)

The Alvarez theory inspired scientists to use computers to simulate the effects of a large impact on Earth's atmosphere. These simulations were later used to predict how a major nuclear war might affect the atmosphere. The term *nuclear winter* was coined to describe the worldwide drop in temperature the simulations predicted would follow such a war.

GEOLOGIC TIME

Scientists who study the evolution of life have divided Earth's history into units called eras and periods. Each of these units is distinguished by distinct planetary conditions and life-forms.

ERA	PERIOD	MILLIONS OF YEARS AGO
Cenozoic	Quaternary	1.8 to present
(Age of Mammals)	Tertiary	65 to 1.8
	CRETACEOUS-TERTIARY (K-T) BOUNDARY	
Mesozoic	Cretaceous	144 to 65
(Age of Reptiles)	Jurassic	206 to 144
	Triassic	248 to 206
	PERMIAN-TRIASSIC (P-T) BOUNDARY	
Paleozoic	Permian	290 to 248
(early animals)	Carboniferous	354 to 290
	Devonian	417 to 354
	Silurian	443 to 417
	Ordovician	490 to 443
	Cambrian	540 to 490

The Alvarezes' theory was controversial when they announced it in 1980. None of the Alvarez team were paleontologists, yet they had proposed a theory of mass extinction, which is the domain of fossil specialists. Astronomers and scientists specializing in various aspects of Earth's atmosphere, chemistry, and physics soon joined the effort to solve the mass-extinction mystery.

An impact large enough to kill off the dinosaurs would have left a crater at least 60 miles in diameter. Yet it seemed that no such crater had been discovered. Of course, if the impact had occurred on the ocean floor, the crater might never be found. That is because the bottom of the ocean is constantly changing. Molten rock from Earth's mantle, the layer of rock that lies below the crust, emerges along ridges in the ocean floor. Meanwhile, solid material falls into the ocean's deep trenches, where it melts and becomes part of the mantle. Robert Dietz coined the term *seafloor spreading* to describe this process. Due to seafloor spreading, about half of the ocean floor of the Cretaceous period has plunged into deep-sea trenches and melted, destroying any craters that might have been present.

Non-impact theories also were offered to explain how concentrations of iridium could form in Earth's crust. In 1981 one researcher proposed that bacteria could have caused the high concentration of iridium in manganese nodules—metallic lumps that form on the seafloor under certain conditions. Could bacterial activity also have caused the K-T boundary?

Some experts insisted that volcanoes produced the K-T iridium. Samples of lava from Hawaii's Kilauea volcano have been shown to contain iridium from Earth's mantle. Perhaps the iridium at the K-T boundary was also volcanic.

But other pro-impact evidence began to emerge in 1983. It came from a study of the osmium found at various K-T impact

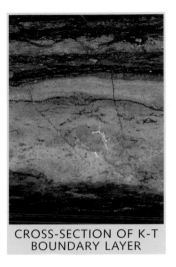

CROSS-SECTION OF K-T
BOUNDARY LAYER

sites. Osmium is a metallic element that, like iridium, is abundant in meteorites but rare in Earth's crust. Osmium from Earth's crust is different from osmium found in meteorites. Scientists thought that the K-T osmium looked meteoritic. Also, the osmium evidence seemed different from site to site. This suggested the possibility of more than one impact.

Reports of unusual iridium concentrations began flowing in from around the world. Then in 1985, researchers reported finding large amounts of carbon in the iridium layer. One source of carbon is fire. The carbon in the iridium layer suggested that vaporizing debris from the impact might have set off extensive wildfires.

Meteorite impacts generate intense heat. Even an ocean impact could produce enough heat to start fires on land more than 600 miles away. A layer of clay found at the K-T boundary in Denmark, Spain, and New Zealand contained a large amount of carbon. The clay layer had been deposited in less than one year—carbon dust could not have stayed in the air longer than that. The amount of carbon found in the K-T impact layers around the world was the same as the amount contained in 10 percent of the world's current plant and animal life.

Fires would contribute to extinction in several ways. Many plants and animals would be burned. The fires would give off poisonous gases, endangering the remaining life on land. Smoke from fires would block sunlight more efficiently than dust would, slowing the growth of the surviving plants. Smoke would also cause a bigger drop in global temperatures than dust alone, and the lower temperatures would last longer.

More K-T impact data soon emerged. Researchers from the U.S. Geological Survey found shocked quartz at the K-T boundary in North America, Europe, Asia, and elsewhere. Then in 1989 a team of Arizona State University scientists led by John McHone reported finding stishovite in the K-T iridium layer in northeast New Mexico, near the Colorado border. Stishovite is known only from experiments, nuclear blasts, and meteorite craters. A few scientists believed the iridium at the K-T boundary came from volcanoes instead of meteorites. But stishovite cannot come from a volcano.

● FINDING THE K-T CRATER

In the late 1980s, scientists could still only guess at the exact location of the K-T impact. The clues led them to the Caribbean Sea. Waves reaching 165 feet or higher had washed over the Gulf of Mexico region at the end of the Cretaceous period, as shown by rocky sediments found near the Brazos River in Texas. Could an impact in a shallow sea somewhere in the Caribbean have generated the waves?

In 1990 a University of Arizona scientist found the K-T impact structure everyone was looking for. It was the gigantic Chicxulub structure, more than 105 miles in diameter, submerged off the northern coast of the Yucatán Peninsula. *Chicxulub* (pronounced CHEEK-shoo-loob) means "tail of the devil" in the Mayan language. Scientists had a devil of a time finding it, too, despite its size.

Oil prospectors had discovered the structure in the 1950s. The prospectors drilled at Chicxulub but found no oil. The structure was forgotten, then rediscovered in 1978 by Antonio

Camargo and Glen Penfield of Mexico's national oil company, Petróleos Mexicanos. They suggested that it was a giant impact structure. But few people outside the oil-exploration business knew about the idea. Only in 1990, when Chicxulub was connected to the K-T impact, did the theory get widespread attention.

Some geologists considered the possibility that more than one impact had triggered an environmental disaster that wiped out the dinosaurs. As many as ten of the impact structures then known in Asia, Africa, the Caribbean, and North America were formed close to the time when the dinosaurs became extinct.

But assigning accurate dates to impact structures can be difficult. Ideally, the rock of which a structure is made contains radioactive elements such as uranium, potassium, or rubidium. Because radioactive elements decay at a predictable rate,

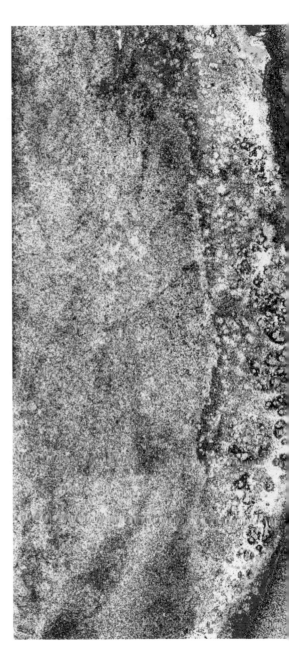

This aerial infrared photograph of the Chicxulub structure shows only a portion of the giant crater.

they can be used to date the rocks in which they are found. If the rock contains no radioactive elements, geologists must make an educated guess. They try to determine the approximate ages of the target rock (the rock at the point where the meteorite hit), the rock underneath the crater, and the rocks that fill the crater. An impact has to be younger than the rocks below it and older than the rocks above it. Unfortunately, the geologic record often is incomplete, making it hard to assign dates to rocks in and around a crater. This results in a wide range of time during which the crater could have formed.

The two craters thought to have formed closest to the time of the dinosaurs' extinction were Chicxulub and a crater near Manson, Iowa. Debris from ice-age glaciers lies atop the Manson structure, which measures more than 21 miles in diameter. The structure was discovered in the 1950s, when water wells were drilled through the glacial debris. The K-T controversy attracted new attention to the Manson structure. Further research showed that it is approximately seventy-four million years old—much older than Chicxulub, which is about sixty-five million years old.

Earth scientists at the Center for Low Radioactivity in Gif-sur-Yvette, France, were among those thinking about multiple impacts and the K-T boundary. In 1993 the center's researchers found impact debris on the floor of the Pacific Ocean, north of the Hawaiian Islands. The debris was about the same age as the Chicxulub crater, but the group doubted that the Chicxulub impact was powerful enough to hurl debris all the way from the Caribbean to the North Pacific. Out came the theory that a second asteroid, this one about 1 mile wide, hit the Pacific Ocean at about the same time as the Chicxulub asteroid hit the Caribbean. Experts reacted with caution and disagreement. Skeptics noted that debris of the type found in the Pacific had turned up all over the world.

A few years later, the Pacific Ocean floor provided another surprise, possibly linked to the asteroid that created the Chicxulub crater. In 1996 a University of California scientist reported finding a meteorite that might have been a piece of the asteroid that caused the dinosaurs' extinction. The meteorite was found in sixty-five-million-year-old sediments in the northwest Pacific. The meteorite, which itself contained iridium, had been buried beneath the K-T boundary layer.

IMPACT PROVEN, CONTROVERSY SUBSIDES

Various arguments have contradicted, supported, or forced changes to the K-T extinction-by-impact theory. For example, crocodiles need a relatively warm living environment. Yet crocodiles survived the K-T extinction, despite the freezing temperatures that a catastrophic impact likely would have produced by clouding the atmosphere. And according to calculations published in 2002 by geologist Kevin Pope, the K-T impact did not send anywhere near enough fine dust into the atmosphere to block sunlight, stop plant growth, and lead to the extinctions observed in the fossil record.

The discovery of dinosaur fossils just above the K-T boundary would settle the question. Unfortunately, while fossils of microscopic life forms called foraminifera are plentiful at the K-T boundary, fossils of larger animals are not. This is not surprising, though, because animals rarely become fossils. Conditions have to be just right or the remains are destroyed. It was possible that no fossils of nonmicroscopic animals would ever be found near the K-T boundary. Yet in 1995, fossil hunters in

Antarctica located the mass graves of a variety of kinds of fish buried just above the K-T band of iridium. The fossil beds do not prove that impact killed the fish found in them. Nor do they prove that the asteroid wiped out all the other animals that went extinct around the world at about the same time. Still, they do point to a catastrophe of some sort.

The fish beds lie far from the Chicxulub impact site. The beds also lie far from the Deccan Traps, a vast area of lava flows in west-central India. The Deccan Traps were produced at the end of the Cretaceous, during a period of volcanic eruptions that were much grander than any seen in the present day. Perhaps the poisonous gases given off by the Indian volcanoes killed the Antarctic fish and other species.

The heavy sulfur content of the rocks at the Chicxulub impact site supports the impact theory, however. Sulfur compounds rocketed into the atmosphere by the asteroid impact would have been light enough to stay suspended in the air for anywhere from ten years to a century—long enough to cause extreme changes in climate. Carbon dust probably would have settled to Earth within six months. That would not have been enough time to bring about a climate change drastic enough to kill off the dinosaurs.

The 1991 eruption of Mt. Pinatubo in the Philippines released 20 million tons of sulfur dioxide into the atmosphere, causing worldwide temperatures to drop slightly. Up to 1 trillion tons of sulfur dioxide would have mushroomed into the sky after the K-T impact—50,000 times as much as Pinatubo released. The sulfur dioxide would have been converted into a thick cloud of sulfuric acid. That cloud might have made temperatures on Earth drop even more than they did in the last ice age.

Mt. Pinatubo's 1991 eruption showed scientists how sulfur dioxide released into Earth's atmosphere affects temperatures and life on our planet.

For much of the twentieth century, most geologists rejected the idea of cosmic impact. It should come as little surprise, then, that many also objected to the idea of mass extinction by cosmic impact. Geologists of the past two centuries clung fiercely to the uniformitarian philosophy. Theories that conflicted with the philosophy were usually ignored or quickly dismissed. At first, the Alvarezes' theory fared no better. It was just too catastrophic to suit most geologists.

The situation has changed with the arrival of the twenty-first century. No one disputes that an impact occurred at the end of the Cretaceous period. And few experts doubt that impact caused or at least contributed to the dinosaurs' extinction.

Chapter 4

IMPACT AND PERIODIC MASS EXTINCTIONS

At least half a dozen mass extinctions have occurred in Earth's history. The one 65 million years ago, between the Cretaceous and Tertiary periods, wiped out as many as seven of every ten species living on Earth at the time. But the mass extinction that took place between the Permian and Triassic periods 250 million years ago was the greatest of them all. It destroyed approximately nine of every ten marine species, and nearly as many on land.

When an asteroid impact was tied to the extinction of the dinosaurs, many scientists began wondering if catastrophic impact might have caused some of the other mass extinctions that have occurred throughout Earth's history. Some experts even thought that cosmic impact might explain the dinosaurs' rise as well as their extinction. But so far, no one has found strong impact evidence for any of these events.

Interesting findings have been made in recent years, however. A 1994 study of plankton found at the Permian-Triassic (P-T) boundary in Canada showed that these microscopic plants and animals died off suddenly. The extinction appeared to have happened in thousands of years, possibly less. It definitely didn't take millions of years, as scientists had believed.

(Left) This fossilized school of fish is a possible indicator of mass extinction.

In 1996 Oregon State University scientists reported finding shocked quartz, a sign of cosmic impact, at the P-T boundary in Australia. In 2000 a Chinese research team provided further data supporting a rapid P-T extinction. It came from rocks in China and a study of more than three hundred oceanic species that disappeared within a few hundred thousand years.

In 2001 University of Washington researcher Luann Becker announced that she had found evidence of an impact in the late Permian period. This impact, Becker and her colleagues said, brought on the P-T extinction by causing massive volcanic eruptions and changes in ocean chemistry, sea levels, and climate.

Becker's team had unearthed carbon molecules called buckyballs in 250-million-year-old sediments in Japan, China, and Hungary. Buckyballs consist of sixty carbon atoms bonded to one another in the shape of the world's tiniest soccer ball. They are also called buckminsterfullerenes, or simply fullerenes. They were named after architect Buckminster Fuller because they look like the geodesic dome, a structure he designed.

Buckyballs had previously turned up at Canada's Sudbury impact site and at the K-T boundary in Denmark, New Zealand, and North America. Chemical analysis showed that the buckyballs had come from outer space. Trapped inside them were certain forms of gases that are rare on Earth but common in meteorites. Enough buckyballs have been found at the P-T boundary to suggest that they were once part of a comet or asteroid measuring up to 7.5 miles in diameter.

Some scientists reacted to Becker's announcement with cautious enthusiasm. Others, however, were more skeptical. No crater of the right size and age to support Becker's idea had yet been found.

After the 1980 Alvarez paper on impact and the dinosaurs was published, scientists found high levels of iridium that they

Researcher Luann Becker displays a model buckyball.

associated with five other mass extinctions, including the P-T extinction. These layers range in age from 590 million to 38 million years. The iridium concentrations are far lower than those at the K-T boundary.

A study published in 1996 casts doubt on the origin of most of the world's iridium layers. According to a scientist at the University of Rochester, in New York, an iridium-rich layer could form without the dust cloud from a large impact. Weathering of smaller meteorites could add iridium to mineral layers. Once a meteorite falls to Earth it begins to break down if exposed to the elements. Iridium weathered from the meteorite would eventually be washed into the oceans and slowly settle onto the seafloor, forming a layer of sediments high in iridium. The only iridium layer that this process cannot explain is the

Early Speculations about the Impact-Extinction Connection

Mass extinction by cosmic impact is not a new idea. Scientist Harvey H. Nininger began thinking about impact and extinction more than sixty years ago. Nininger was one of the greatest meteorite hunters of all time. In 1937 asteroid Hermes passed within 480,000 miles of Earth, about twice the distance from Earth to the Moon. Taking notice of Hermes, Nininger published an article in 1942 discussing the idea that asteroid impact caused Earth's geologic revolutions. These major geologic changes were chaotic. Climates changed. Sea levels shifted. Volcanoes went wild. New species abruptly replaced old ones. Nininger was one of the few scientists who used impact to try to explain these geologic revolutions.

Digby McLaren was another. A respected scientist, McLaren wondered if impact might have caused the mass extinction about 365 million years ago, in the late Devonian period. That extinction was one of the most extensive in the history of life on Earth. Over a 20-million-year period, about seven out of every ten marine animals died off. Three sizeable craters are known to have formed around the end of the Devonian: Alamo in Nevada, Charlevoix in Canada, and Siljan in Sweden. Each is more than 30 miles in diameter. McLaren spoke of the impact-extinction idea in his presidential address to the Paleontological Society in 1970.

one at the K-T boundary. The K-T boundary layer contains one thousand times more iridium than is found in all of the world's oceans. Its formation would require the weathering of far too many meteorites in a limited period of time.

In 1984 McLaren was a member of a research team at Los Alamos National Laboratory in New Mexico. The group found evidence that seemed to support his impact-extinction idea. The evidence was an iridium layer in northwestern Australia that had formed in the late Devonian.

There was some doubt, however, about the meaning of the Australian iridium. It was found only in fossil bacteria. This suggested that the iridium layer formed as a result of a normal biological process. If so, it had probably not come from a meteorite. Besides, the extinction in the late Devonian had occurred over a twenty-million-year period. Surely an impact would have caused a much faster extinction.

Nobel Prize-winning American chemist Harold C. Urey took his turn at mass-extinction theory too. Urey knew that Earth and the Moon had absorbed many impacts early in the history of the solar system. He considered the possibility that comets had collided with Earth throughout its history. In 1957 Urey published a theory connecting tektites to the collisions of comets with Earth. Urey compared the ages of various tektite strewnfields with the ages of the most recent, relatively minor mass extinctions that occurred from one million to thirty-six million years ago. The ages agreed fairly well.

In 1973 Urey calculated the energy an object the size of Halley's comet would release if it hit Earth. He figured it would be enough to raise global temperatures and bring about earthquakes that would in turn cause lava flows. Urey even suspected that the dinosaurs had fallen victim to a comet's impact, long before evidence for the idea emerged.

⚙ DID IMPACT GIVE THE DINOSAURS THEIR BIG CHANCE?

No one has found any iridium marking the beginning of the dinosaurs' reign. Neverthless, some experts suspect a link between impact and the evolutionary success of the dinosaurs.

Dinosaurs appeared on Earth during the Triassic period, which ended about two hundred million years ago. Before the dinosaurs came on the scene, giant reptiles dominated life on Earth. Paleontologists once believed that dinosaurs grabbed the advantage from the reptiles over millions of years in a classic struggle for survival. But recent evidence suggests that the dinosaurs took over more quickly than that. And the takeover might have had more to do with luck than with biological superiority.

During the late Triassic period, Earth had one just great continent—Pangaea. Giant reptiles dominated the landscape, but dinosaurs grew to only the size of a house cat. Even the dragonflies of the period, with their 3-foot wingspans, were more impressive than the dinosaurs.

Then, possibly, Earth was hit by a devastating cosmic impact. Or perhaps the climate changed as geologic forces broke Pangaea into smaller continents. Whatever the cause, a mass extinction ravaged the planet, killing one of every two species on Earth. A 2001 study led by the University of Washington's Peter Ward revealed that the extinction occurred rapidly, in fifty thousand years or less. With many other species out of the way, the dinosaurs must have quickly adapted to fill suddenly unoccupied ecological roles.

The Manicouagan impact may have given the dinosaurs the lucky break they needed to become dominant. The Manicouagan structure in Quebec, Canada, measures about 62 miles in diameter. It formed about 214 million years ago, toward the end of the Triassic period.

American geologists working near Corfino in northern Italy found shocked quartz in three separate rock layers deposited about 200 million years ago, at the end of the Triassic period. The shocked quartz suggested that three cosmic impacts shook Earth during the late Triassic, over a period of hundreds of thousands of years. But they occurred millions of years after the Manicouagan impact, which also seemed too small to bring about the global Triassic-Jurassic extinction, one of the largest on record.

MANICOUAGAN STRUCTURE

Eastern North America has extensive solidified lava flows called basalts that formed in the late Triassic, about 210 million years ago. The basalts appear throughout the Newark Supergroup, a rock formation that extends from Newfoundland on the North Atlantic coast to Florida in the south. Maybe the volcanoes that made the basalts caused the extinction. It appears that volcanic rocks found in Europe, West Africa, and South America, as well as the Atlantic Coast lavas, all erupted from a vast system of volcanoes over a few million years at the end of the Triassic period. At that time, Europe, Africa, North America, and South America were connected to one another as part of the Pangaean supercontinent. Geologic forces would soon begin to break Pangaea apart, slowly pushing the continents to their present-day locations.

Maybe volcanoes were also to blame for the extinction at the end of the Permian period. In the late Permian, lava flooded out of volcanoes in Siberia, Russia, for one million years. A cloud of sulfur oxide sent into the atmosphere by the volcanoes could have led to deadly showers of acid rain. Or, if the cloud blocked out sunlight, a period of global cooling could have begun.

Robert Dietz speculated that asteroid impacts might have caused both the extinctions and the massive lava flows at the end of the Permian and Triassic periods. He thought that the force of an impact occurring near a vein of magma close to Earth's surface could cause underground volcanic activity. His candidate impact site for the Siberian volcanism was nearby Noril'sk, which looked to him suspiciously like Sudbury in Canada. He theorized that the North American basalts could have been caused by an impact somewhere in the Bahama Islands, in the South Atlantic. These ideas have never been proven.

Other scientists have suggested that impact-generated volcanism helped do in the dinosaurs. They theorized that shock waves from a giant impact, traveling through Earth's crust, came together to release an outpouring of lava on exactly the opposite side of Earth from the impact site. The late Cretaceous did leave behind the giant Chicxulub crater in Central America and a huge lava field— India's Deccan Traps. But geologists have reconstructed where the continents sat sixty-five million years ago. Chicxulub and the Deccan Traps were not on opposite sides of Earth.

Let us assume that cosmic impact did indeed cause many of Earth's mass extinctions. What could have brought on all of these catastrophic impacts? Even geologists who favor a link between mass extinctions and impact have tended to think of impacts as random events.

Then it was suggested that impact and extinction might be part of a grand cosmic cycle. This idea is known as the Shiva hypothesis, named for the Hindu god of destruction and birth. This theme came from the work of David Raup and J. John Sepkoski Jr.

During the early 1980s, the two University of Chicago paleontologists ran computer analyses on thousands of extinct organisms. Their analyses showed that major extinctions have swept Earth once every 26 million years over the last 250 million years.

Two paleontologists at Princeton University, in New Jersey, had published a similar finding in 1977. Combining geological, paleontological, and chemical evidence, they had concluded that extinctions had taken place once every 32 million years over the past 250 million years. At the time, most paleontologists found the idea hard to swallow. For one thing, the Princeton researchers had no solid ideas about what could be causing the periodic extinctions. The same problem stumped Raup and Sepkoski in the 1980s. No earthbound explanation seemed

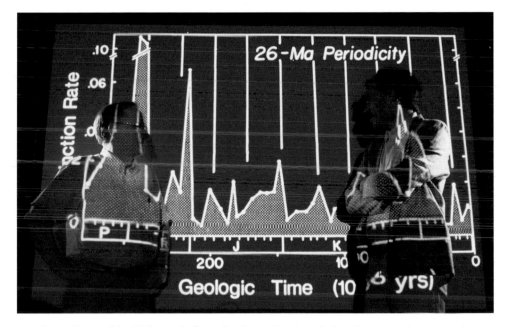

Dr. Raup (left) and Dr. Sepkoski stand in front of a graph that illustrates their theory of periodic mass extinction.

possible for events that happened over such vast periods of time. They would need help from astronomers.

● COSMIC CYCLES OF EXTINCTION

Three astronomical theories of mass extinction came out in 1984 and 1985. One stated that the motion of the solar system through the galaxy caused mass extinction cycles. The second theory blamed the extinctions on an undiscovered companion star to the Sun. The third theory depended on the existence of an undiscovered planet beyond Pluto.

Reseachers had previously suggested that the Sun slowly travels up and down through the rotating spiral disk of our galaxy. Every thirty-one to thirty-three million years, according to the theory, the solar system would pass through or near a cloud of gas and dust at the halfway point of its journey—in the galactic plane, an imaginary plane running the length and width of the galaxy.

One version of the galactic plane theory depends on the Oort cloud, a vast sphere of comets that encircles the solar system. According to this version of the theory, each time the solar system passes through the galactic plane, the interstellar dust cloud's gravity slings a group of comets from the Oort cloud toward Earth's neighborhood. Several of the comets strike Earth, and mass extinction follows. A second version of the theory proposes that electromagnetic and cosmic rays become more intense near the middle of the galactic plane. Exposure to these intense rays might cause climate change on Earth.

Unfortunately, the galactic plane theory's timing seems to be off. The Sun now sits fairly close to the galactic plane, which means that a mass extinction should be imminent or should have recently occurred. But the most recent mass extinction took place about eleven million years ago. This means Earth should be approximately halfway between extinction events.

No companion star to the Sun has yet been found, but space scientists have discussed the possibility. They have proposed that a nearby, dim star much smaller than the Sun passes through the Oort cloud about once every twenty-six million years. The encounter frees comets from the Oort cloud. Some later collide with Earth over a one-million-year period.

The theoretical companion star is sometimes called Nemesis, after the Greek goddess of vengeance. Nemesis would have to orbit about 2 light-years from the Sun—much closer than any other star. Still, its small size and dimness would make Nemesis difficult for astronomers to find.

This theory has a problem, too. The gravitational tug of passing stars could prevent Nemesis from remaining in orbit around the Sun long enough to cause a series of mass extinctions. Eugene Shoemaker estimated that the chance Nemesis actually exists is no better than one in one thousand.

The theory about an undiscovered tenth planet—planet X—explains one astronomical problem that has nothing to do with periodic extinction. It explains what upsets comets from their orbit in the Kuiper belt. The Kuiper belt is a disk of tens of thousands of comets that lies beyond the orbit of Neptune, more than 4 billion miles from the Sun. Distant as it is, it is only one-hundredth as far from the Sun as the Oort cloud is. The existence of the Kuiper belt was proposed to explain the origin of short-period comets. These comets complete an orbit of the Sun in less than two hundred years. They travel along the plane of the ecliptic, the plane in which the planets are found.

For decades, scientists had only theoretical evidence for the Kuiper belt. Starting in 1992, astronomers using ground-based telescopes began spotting large, icy objects in the outer solar system. By 1995 twenty-three such objects had been identified, most more than 60 miles in diameter. Then the Hubble Space Telescope captured images of thirty smaller objects. These were 3.5 to 6 miles in diameter, about the size of Halley's comet.

By 2002, astronomers knew of more than five hundred Kuiper belt objects. If planet X swept through the Kuiper belt once every twenty-eight million years, its gravity would eject some of these objects out of the solar system. But other objects would head toward Earth as comets. The ones that got in Earth's way would, in theory, leave a cluster of craters every twenty-eight million years. Do crater ages bear out this theory? Walter Alvarez and Richard A. Muller, one of Alvarez's colleagues at the University of California, Berkeley, said yes.

Alvarez and Muller analyzed the ages of impact craters that were more than 6 miles in diameter and between 5 million and 250 million years old. The study showed a cycle of impacts every 28.5 million years. The crater clusters generally agreed in age with Raup and Sepkoski's list of extinctions. But according

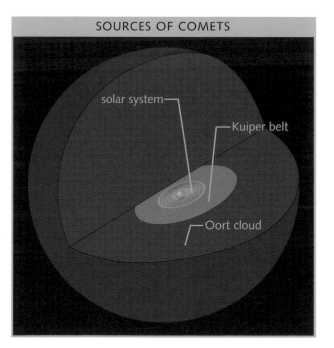

This diagram shows the layers of the Kuiper belt and Oort cloud.

to one expert, crater ages are too uncertain to reveal any such patterns. And most astronomers doubt that planet X exists.

SPIRAL ARMS AND EXPLODING STARS

Many scientists regard astronomical theories for mass extinction as highly controversial. Although these theories are newer than the concept of cosmic impact, they have been around for decades.

Otto Schindewolf, at the University of Tübingen in Germany, published an astronomical extinction theory in 1962. Schindewolf offered the idea that the heat and radiation produced by a supernova (an exploding star) brought about the P-T extinction. He was one of the world's great experts on the late Permian extinction. Still, his supernova theory faced opposition. When Schindewolf died in 1972, his theory was still controversial.

Two scientists at England's Royal Observatory published an astronomical extinction theory in 1979. They thought the Sun's passage through the spiral arms of the Milky Way galaxy might explain mass extinctions and the ice ages. The solar system could encounter other clouds of comets like the Oort cloud on its travels within the arms, each of which contains millions of stars. The frequency of impacts on Earth would rise on each passage through the densest part of the galaxy.

In 1995 two researchers published a theory that gave Schindewolf's supernova theory new life. The researchers showed how a supernova 30 light-years away could destroy Earth's ozone layer—the layer of the atmosphere that blocks most of the Sun's ultraviolet radiation. The destruction of the ozone layer would expose organisms to potentially deadly levels of radiation.

The exact cause of the Permian extinction remains uncertain, but stay tuned. Who knows what the next discovery will bring?

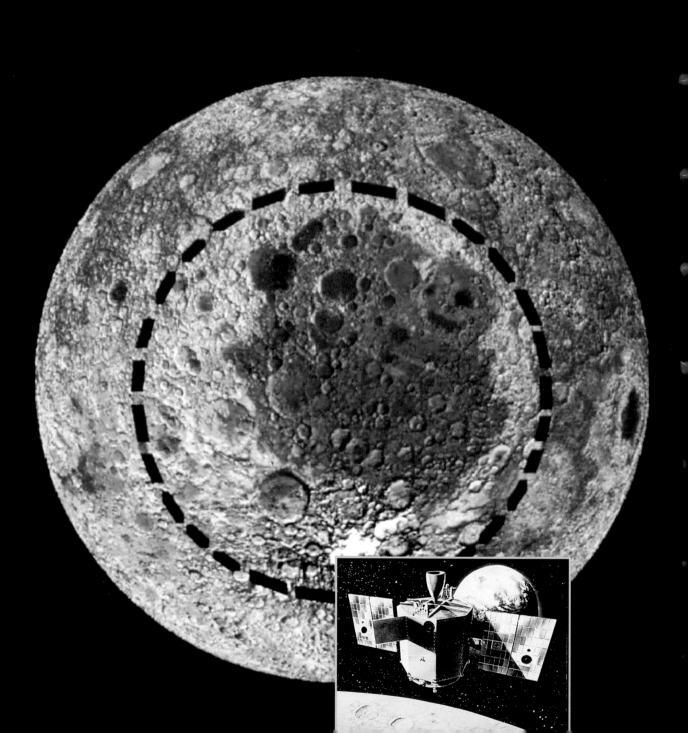

Chapter 5

IMPACT, THE PLANETS, AND THE ORIGIN OF LIFE ON EARTH

No object in the solar system is safe from the destructive power of cosmic bombs. Cosmic collisions have shaped many of Earth's neighbors and even gave birth to the Moon.

The idea that the Moon was formed after an object the size of Mars (4,200 miles in diameter) crashed into Earth was first proposed in 1975. According to the theory, debris from the collision came together to form the Moon. Computer simulations and data collected from the Moon by the *Clementine* space probe in 1994 breathed new life into the theory. The *Clementine* data were analyzed to determine the aluminum and iron content of the Moon. The results fit the idea that the Moon formed from an ocean of lava that once covered Earth.

Most planetary scientists came to accept the theory that a giant impact created the Moon. Nevertheless, they found it difficult to see how a single impact could have created the Moon and set it in its orbit around Earth. A complicated computer simulation solved the problem in 2001.

The Moon itself is covered with craters. The largest, the South Pole-Aitken Basin, is 1,550 miles in diameter. It would stretch from Los Angeles, California, to Houston, Texas.

(Left) This view of the Moon shows the South Pole-Aitken Basin. **(Inset)** The *Clementine* space probe

Historical Lunar Impacts

The collision of comet Shoemaker-Levy 9 with Jupiter in 1994 may not have been the first impact that humans have witnessed. A group of English monks may have seen a lunar impact on June 18, 1178.

Jack B. Hartung of the State University of New York at Stony Brook based this claim on an account by the medieval English writer Gervase of Canterbury. Gervase reported a strange phenomenon witnessed by half a dozen monks as they gazed at a thin crescent Moon one evening. The monks saw a series of sparks and flames divide the upper tip of the Moon. The visible portion of the Moon seemed to throb. Then it went dark.

Did the monks witness the creation of a new crater? Hartung said they did, and it would have been crater Giordano Bruno. Giordano Bruno, 12.4 miles in diameter, is a young crater. Lunar erosion has not yet erased the fine rays of impact debris that radiate from it. Some of Hartung's colleagues, however, believe that the monks saw a fireball falling to Earth, with the Moon in their line of sight behind it. Of course, this theory doesn't explain why the monks saw a series of lights.

The odds certainly are against Hartung's theory. By counting craters, scientists have estimated that a large object hits the Moon only once every one hundred thousand years. Hartung himself admitted that the

Beginning in the 1960s, NASA probes provided evidence of impact craters on Mercury, Venus, and Mars and both of its moons. For example, Mars has an impact crater, Hellas Basin, with an average diameter of 1,100 miles.

In 1974 and 1975, the *Mariner 10* space probe took pictures of about half the surface of Mercury, the planet nearest the chances of a lunar impact happening during the three-thousand-year period of human history were only one in one thousand. The chances that a human would see such an impact were even slimmer. The impact would, after all, just as likely hit the far side of the Moon as the side facing human observers.

A crater-forming impact on any rocky body would cause the body to wobble for a time. If a major lunar impact occurred eight hundred years ago, the Moon would still be wobbling slightly. Scientists have measured such a wobble by bouncing a laser beam off mirrors placed on the Moon by *Apollo* astronauts. But at least one expert suspects that forces inside the Moon, not impact, caused the wobble.

Another expert has argued that about 10,000,000 tons of debris would have been ejected by the impact, leading to a spectacular, week-long meteor storm visible from virtually every continent on Earth in late June 1178. Ancient records faithfully record other meteoric events, but it appears that no one made note of a spectacular meteor storm that month.

The first confirmed observations of lunar impacts took place on the evening of November 17, 1999, during the Leonid meteor storm. Amateur astronomers in North America independently videotaped or saw six small impacts on the night (dark) side of the Moon. Size estimates of the impacting bodies ranged from 1 or 2 feet in diameter to much smaller.

Sun. The images revealed many craters, including the giant Caloris Basin, which is about 800 miles in diameter. The impact that caused it would have sent shock waves all the way through the planet. These shock waves may have caused the hills, valleys, and broken-looking craters that cover much of the surface on exactly the opposite side of the planet from the Caloris Basin.

Jupiter, Saturn, Uranus, and Neptune are gaseous planets, with no solid surface. They show no permanent signs of impact. But all four of these planets have solid moons. The *Voyager* probes found craters on these moons—sometimes in large numbers.

Impact evidence comes from as far away as Pluto. In the early 1990s, the Hubble Space Telescope took images of Pluto and its moon, Charon, that hinted at a catastrophic collision. Scientists expected Charon to follow a circular orbit around Pluto, as other planets' moons do. Instead, the images showed that Charon follows an oval-shaped orbit. A collision between either Pluto or Charon and a chunk of space debris could have changed Charon's orbit. If so, the collision happened within the past ten million years. Given more time, Pluto's gravity would have pulled Charon back into a more nearly circular orbit.

How big was the collision? Pluto measures approximately 2,000 miles in diameter, about the size of the Moon. Scientists estimate that an object hitting Pluto would have to be at least 155 miles wide to change Pluto's orbit. A smaller, but still massive, object hitting Charon could change the moon's orbit.

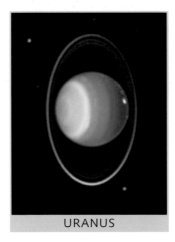
URANUS

Giant impacts may also have taken place elsewhere in the solar system. They might have knocked Uranus over on its side and set Venus, Uranus, and Pluto rotating in a direction opposite that of the other planets.

Uranus, the seventh planet from the Sun, is the only planet in the solar system whose axis is nearly horizontal compared to its orbit. Uranus's axis slants 82 degrees from the vertical. Earth, by comparison, tilts only 23 degrees, enough to produce changing seasons. Impact may have caused Uranus's unusual tilt.

Uranus is nearly 32,000 miles in diameter. The object that theoretically knocked over Uranus would have had to be about the size of Earth—approximately 8,000 miles in diameter.

Uranus, Pluto, and Venus (the second planet from the Sun) are the only planets in the solar system that have a retrograde rotation. This means that they rotate in a clockwise direction as viewed from above the planet's north pole. All the other planets in the solar system have prograde rotation: they rotate counterclockwise. No one knows why these three planets rotate backward compared to the others, but collision with massive objects might explain it.

Saturn, the sixth planet from the Sun, has more than thirty moons, including the oddballs Mimas and Tethys. Mimas gets its strange appearance from the crater Herschel, which makes the moon look as if it has a single giant eye. Mimas is nearly 242 miles in diameter. Herschel, at 80 miles in diameter, covers more than one tenth of the surface of Mimas. If the impact that produced Herschel had been any more powerful, Mimas would likely have been destroyed. The crater Odysseus on Tethys is even larger than Herschel. Odysseus stretches 248 miles across on a moon that measures 657 miles in diameter.

Two of Saturn's smallest moons, Janus and Epimethus, orbit only 31 miles apart. Scientists think that an impact may have split a larger body apart to form these moons. Something similar probably happened to twelve other Saturnian moons. These tiny moons orbit in three or four clusters. This leads astronomers to speculate that the twelve moons likely were formed when cosmic bombs blasted three or four larger moons.

● A STAR IS BORN

Cosmic bombs have been a force for creation as well as for destruction. The three basic ingredients needed for life are a steady energy source, water, and organic compounds (chemicals containing carbon atoms). Cometary impacts could have provided the chemicals needed for life early in Earth's history. They could have done the same for Europa, one of Jupiter's moons, which may hide an ocean—and possibly life—beneath its icy crust.

The solar system probably was born after a slowly rotating cloud of gas and dust collapsed under the force of its own gravity. While the Sun began to heat up at the center, the cloud flattened into a disk. Dust particles floating in the disk collided and stuck together. Clumps of particles grew larger and larger, eventually becoming asteroid-sized objects called planetesimals. The planetesimals, in turn, merged to form the rocky planets of Mercury, Venus, Earth, and Mars. Farther away from the Sun, gases formed into the planets Jupiter, Saturn, Uranus, and Neptune. The leftover debris in the outer part of the disk gave rise to Pluto and the comets in the Kuiper belt.

Much of the debris that swirled about the early solar system—comets—continued to collide with Earth during its first billion years. During this time, comets may have delivered water to Earth, along with the molecular seeds from which life blossomed. Scientists had speculated since the 1950s that the water in Earth's oceans came from comets, but there was one problem. The chemical composition of seawater was different from that of all known comets. The comets contained more deuterium, a heavy form of hydrogen, than Earth water does. But in May 2001, scientists at NASA's Goddard Space Flight Center in Greenbelt, Maryland, announced that comet LINEAR probably had a composition similar to Earth water.

Comet LINEAR broke into several pieces and then disappeared during the summer of 2000. Using telescopes situated high atop Mauna Kea, Hawaii, scientists determined the composition of LINEAR before it vanished. They did so by measuring the frequencies of infrared light that the comet's molecules emitted. (Different molecules give off different frequencies of light.) The scientists found that LINEAR contained less carbon monoxide, methane, ethane, and acetylene than other known comets. They thought it probably also contained less deuterium than other comets, but they were unable to verify this.

Laboratory experiments suggest that carbon monoxide, ethane, and acetylene molecules formed at low temperatures such as those found near Neptune's orbit. Therefore most comets probably formed in the outer part of the solar system. But LINEAR's chemical composition included less of these compounds. LINEAR could have formed much closer to the Sun, possibly near Jupiter's orbit, where temperatures would have been too warm for these molecules to freeze into the comet's ices. The same experiments also show that a comet

This series of photographs shows how comet LINEAR began to break up while traveling through space.

formed under warmer conditions would have lower concentrations of deuterium, like seawater on Earth.

Once the comets had formed billions of years ago, Jupiter's intense gravity would have flung many of them into the Oort cloud in the distant reaches of the solar system. Likewise, Jupiter would have sent other comets on a collision course with Earth. These comets could have delivered organic molecules to Earth.

Evidence for this idea came with the discovery of extraterrestrial amino acids in the Murchison meteorite that fell in Australia in 1969. Amino acids are the building blocks of proteins, molecules that carry out the processes of life. Before the Murchison meteorite was found, it had seemed impossible that any organic compounds could have survived the formation of the solar system.

The discovery started a controversy. One group of scientists argued that the amino acids could easily have rubbed off the fingertips of the people who had touched the meteorite. But another group believed that the amino acids had formed in outer space.

In 1987 a team of scientists from Arizona State University and the California Institute of Technology proved that the amino acids had formed in outer space. The amino acids contained unusually high amounts of deuterium, which is rare on Earth. Deuterium is abundant, however, in the cosmic dust from which solar systems are made.

The discovery of buckyballs at the Sudbury impact site further backed up the theory that comets and asteroids delivered the seeds of life to Earth. At first scientists thought that the buckyballs might have formed during the impact. But a research team from the University of Rochester in New York and Scripps Institution of Oceanography in California proved that the buckyballs had come from space. Preserved inside them was a form of helium that is common in meteorites.

The Sudbury buckyballs show that organic compounds could have survived space travel and the violence of a catastrophic impact. The Sudbury asteroid apparently protected the buckyballs from radiation and other destructive cosmic forces during an outer space journey that took billions of years.

Laboratory simulations suggest that organic molecules could also survive the violence of a comet crashing into a planet. A comet colliding head-on with Earth would generate rock-melting temperatures of 18,000 degrees Fahrenheit. The explosion following the impact would cause pressures of 1,000,000 atmospheres. Such a collision, many scientists believe, would vaporize most of the comet, along with any organic molecules that it might carry. But if a comet struck Earth at a low angle instead of head-on, the collision would be much less violent. It would produce cooler temperatures of 1,800 degrees Fahrenheit and weaker pressures of 200,000 atmospheres.

A team of scientists led by geologist Jennifer Blank at the University of California, Berkeley, subjected five types of amino acids to 200,000 atmospheres of impact pressure. The experiments were conducted with a stainless steel cannon that shot a plastic cylinder about the size of a soda can. The projectile reached a speed of 3,600 miles an hour before smashing into a nickel-sized steel container of amino acids sitting in a tank at the end of the cannon's muzzle. A substantial amount of each of the amino acids survived the impact. Some even hooked together into peptides, which are chains of two, three, or four amino acids.

Since Blank's team conducted its experiments, other researchers have discovered evidence that the ingredients of life came from outer space. A study at the NASA Ames Research Center near San Francisco, California, found traces of sugar and related substances in the Murchison meteorite from Australia and the Murray meteorite from Kentucky. Sugar, a substance critical to the formation of life on Earth, had never before been found in a meteorite.

Scientists working at NASA's Johnson Space Center in Houston, Texas, have found a new type of organic material in the Tagish Lake meteorite from Canada. This material consists of hollow organic globules (tiny balls) that could have protected developing organisms early in Earth's history. Earlier, scientists at NASA Ames had made similar globules in experiments that simulated conditions in interstellar space soon after the birth of the solar system.

● ROCKS FROM MARS

If cosmic bombs did deliver the seeds of life to Earth, they could have done the same for Mars. It is also possible that life sprang into existence on Mars first, then was transferred to Earth via cosmic bombs. This theory arose out of the controversy surrounding the martian meteorite ALH84001.

Twenty-eight martian meteorites have been identified so far. Most of them were found in Antarctica. The Antarctic ice sheet flows along the ground like a conveyor belt, depositing meteorites in certain areas. The wind gradually wears away the ice, exposing the meteorites. The dark stones make easy pickings against the white ground.

Many martian meteorites belong the shergottite-nakhlite-chassignite (SNC) category of meteorites. The name refers to the locations where three of the specimens were found: Shergotty, India; Nakhla, Egypt; and Chassigny, France. In conversation, meteorite experts refer to SNC meteorites as "snicks."

Gases trapped in SNCs are chemically similar to the martian atomosphere. The age of the SNCs also points to Mars. Most meteorites are about 4.5 billion years old. The SNCs are mostly only 200 million to 1.3 billion years old. They show signs of volcanic activity. Planetary geologists say that Mars could have been volcanically active when the SNCs formed.

The fist-sized ALH84001 is the most famous martian meteorite. It is so named because it was found in the Allan Hills region of Antarctica, and it was the first specimen catalogued by U.S. scientists in 1984. It gained fame in 1996, when scientists announced that the meteorite contained evidence that Mars may have been home to primitive life-forms 3.6 billion years ago. A team led by scientists at NASA's Johnson Space Center said ALH84001 contained organic molecules, minerals characteristic of biological activity, and structures that were possibly fossils of primitive, bacteria-like organisms.

Most scientists consider the evidence found in ALH84001 too weak to prove whether life once existed on Mars. Samples

Scientists examined meteorite ALH84001 whole (above), then cut it apart (left) to examine its internal structure.

of rock from Mars will probably have to be examined closely to settle the matter. Yet other martian meteorites have already provided hints of what might be found. These meteorites show that Mars may once have had a sea with a composition much like that of Earth's oceans—a sea that might have sustained life.

An analysis of the Nakhla meteorite conducted at Arizona State University (ASU) showed it to be high in chlorine and sodium. These elements are abundant in seawater. Perhaps the chlorine and sodium in the Nakhla meteorite were deposited there as a martian sea evaporated, according to ASU's Carleton Moore.

● ORGANIC STEW

It once appeared that the beginning of life on Earth had nothing to do with cosmic impact. In 1953 Stanley Miller, a graduate student of Harold C. Urey at the University of Chicago, conducted a groundbreaking experiment. For years it would influence thinking about the origin of life.

At that time, chemists believed that Earth's early atmosphere consisted of ammonia, methane, and water vapor. So Miller set up a sealed flask containing these compounds. He then passed an electrical charge through the flask to simulate lightning. Sure enough, amino acids and other organic compounds formed in the flask. The experiment led most scientists to conclude that the early Earth must have been rich in organic compounds.

The origin of life on Earth nevertheless remains a mystery. Scientists once believed that Earth formed under cold conditions. Under this scenario, iron on Earth's surface would have chemically prevented the formation of carbon dioxide. But atmospheric chemists have come to believe that the atmosphere of the early Earth was more like the present atmosphere, which is rich in carbon dioxide, than scientists like Miller and Urey had supposed. Heat produced by cosmic impact would have caused iron to melt and sink to Earth's core. There it would have been unable to keep carbon dioxide from forming. And amino acids are unlikely to form in environments high in carbon dioxide.

No matter how life formed on Earth, it had already become well established by the time of the Sudbury and Vredefort impacts about 2 billion years ago. The earliest fossil bacteria date back to 3.46 billion years ago. The earliest chemical evidence for life goes back farther still, to 3.85 billion years ago. In fact, life may have developed more than once during Earth's early history. But perhaps almost as quickly as life could begin to sprout, a giant comet or asteroid would come along and destroy it.

The oldest known impact took place nearly 3.5 billion years ago. Scientists have yet to find the crater. But they do have geologic evidence from South Africa and Australia leading them to believe that a meteorite much larger than the one that produced the K-T impact crashed somewhere on Earth at that time. Their evidence is a layer of impact spherules (tiny spherical bodies) 8 to 12 inches thick. The layer of spherules from the K-T impact is less than 1 inch thick.

Earth endured larger and more frequent impacts after its birth than it does today. The formation of the solar system left trillions of comets and other debris swirling through space. For seven hundred million years the impact storm continued. Finally it calmed. Fewer and smaller asteroids and comets slammed into Earth. But some of the ones that did find their way to Earth were still large enough to affect the evolution of life. Future cosmic bombs could do likewise, unless humans find a way to disarm them.

Chapter 6

THE CONTINUING THREAT

The chances that any given person on Earth will be killed by a cosmic bomb in any one year are about the same as the odds of dying in any one commercial plane flight. These odds may seem too high. While people do periodically die in airline crashes, no human has ever been killed by a meteorite impact, as far as we know. But that is because humans have lived on Earth for only a short time compared to the frequency of catastrophic impacts. Even an impact that affects only part of Earth is unlikely to occur in a person's lifetime. Still, if a globally destructive impact happens—and it will, every five hundred thousand years or so—it will kill a large percentage of the planet's population. These huge, rare events drive up the odds.

An impact striking water will be just as deadly as one that hits land. Computer simulations performed at Los Alamos National Laboratory show how devastating an ocean impact could be. An iron asteroid measuring 0.6 mile in diameter and traveling at 45,000 miles an hour would send water soaring 12 miles into the atmosphere following such an impact. A wall of water would race in all directions from the impact site at 380 miles an hour. It would reach a height of more than 0.5 mile, threatening to flood coastal cities far from the impact site.

(Left) A NASA artist created this illustration of what a catastrophic meteor impact might look like.

Many small impact events have occurred in recent times. In the twentieth century, Siberia experienced two relatively small but still powerful impact events.

TARGET: SIBERIA

A cosmic bomb shook the Tunguska region of central Siberia at about 7:30 A.M. on June 30, 1908. Residents of northern Russia saw a fireball streak across a clear sky. Then they heard an explosion and felt the blast of a shock wave. Fortunately, the impact site was in an unpopulated area. An immediate search to find the impacting meteorite failed. In 1921 Leonidas A. Kulik, the meteorite expert at the Mineralogical Museum in Petrograd (now St. Petersburg), Russia, began piecing the evidence together. It took Kulik until 1927 to mount his first expedition to Tunguska.

When Kulik finally reached the impact site he found widespread devastation. The impacting object had exploded about 5 miles above the ground, flattening the forest for hundreds of square miles. It unleashed more power than the largest hydrogen bomb. Scientists still debate whether the object that caused the blast was a comet or an asteroid, although it is thought unlikely that a comet could penetrate so deep into Earth's atmosphere.

A second cosmic missile pierced the skies of Siberia over the Sikhote-Alin Mountains on February 12, 1947. The Sikhote-Alin object also fell into a vast wilderness, but it did far less damage than the one at Tunguska. When researchers finally reached the Sikhote-Alin impact site, they found two hundred small craters and many meteorites. One weighed nearly 2 tons.

Most of us are unlikely to experience anything so large as Tunguska or Sikhote-Alin. Impacts similar to Tunguska will occur only about once every one thousand years. A Canadian

The Tunguska impact in Siberia leveled trees for miles around. These trees all point away from the impact.

study led by the University of Western Ontario's Peter Brown indicated, however, that Earth is likely to experience an asteroid impact causing serious regional damage about once every century. Such an asteroid would pack destructive energy equivalent to about 1,000,000 tons of TNT. (The bomb that destroyed Hiroshima, Japan, at the end of World War II produced an explosion equivalent to 15,000 tons of TNT.) Brown's study, published in 2002, was based on more than eight years of data collected by U.S. nuclear monitoring satellites.

Hundreds more meteors explode in the atmosphere each year with the energy of at least 1,000 tons of TNT. Humans rarely witness these explosions. Military satellites, however, record them often. For years, the data remained a military secret. Then, in 1993, the U.S. Department of Defense released the data for 1975 to 1992. During this period, military satellites recorded 136 atmospheric explosions packed with the force of 1,000 or more tons of TNT. This number is low compared to the total number of explosions. Some are over too quickly to be detected. Others are ignored because defense technicians can tell that they are meteors rather than bombs.

The U.S. Air Force no longer makes a secret of its data on atmospheric explosions of meteors. Scientists therefore learned about the great atmospheric meteor explosion of February 1, 1994, soon after it happened. On that day, a meteor entered the atmosphere above Micronesia, a group of islands in the western Pacific Ocean. The meteor shattered into pieces before it disappeared in a brilliant flash. The power of the explosion was equal to that of 100,000 tons of TNT, or nearly seven times the energy of the bomb that destroyed Hiroshima. Fortunately, the explosion took place at an altitude of more than 13 miles. It did no damage at ground level.

◉ A RAIN OF COSMIC FLUFF

Thousands of tons of nearly invisible meteoric dust particles settle to the ground all around us each year. An estimated twenty-six thousand meteorites the size of a pea or larger annually survive their fiery passage through the atmosphere to Earth's surface. Most stream to Earth unnoticed. Meteorites pose little danger to life on Earth, but sometimes they do find living targets.

The Nakhla meteorite that fell in Egypt in 1911 was said to have killed a dog, but this often-repeated story apparently is untrue. *Meteorite* magazine reported in August 1998 that efforts to verify the story were unsuccessful.

The only verified animal death caused by a meteorite occurred on October 15, 1972. On this date, according to *Meteorite* magazine, a cow was killed by a meteorite on a farm near Trujillo, Venezuela. There may have been at least one other such fatality, however. A meteorite found near Brunflo, Sweden, may have killed a nautiloid—a shelled marine creature—during the Ordovician period, about 460 million years ago. The nautiloid and the 2-inch meteorite were preserved together in the sediments of a shallow sea.

Historical documents from places around the world, including China, Italy, the United States, and Iran, have reported human deaths from falling meteorites. Modern authorities question the accuracy of these reports, however. Still, meteorites have been known to injure people. A 10-pound meteorite badly bruised a woman's hand and side in Sylacagua, Alabama, after it punched a hole in the roof of her home on November 30, 1954. The projectiles also damage cars and homes with some regularity.

Meteorites also occasionally pose a risk to satellites and spacecraft. In 1993, for example, NASA postponed the launch of the space shuttle *Discovery* because astronomers had predicted an unusually intense Perseid meteor shower. Skywatchers have comet Swift-Tuttle to thank for the Perseids. They light up the sky by the hundreds each August as Earth passes through the track of ice and dust left behind by the comet. Swift-Tuttle's orbit brings it near Earth's orbit every 130 years; its most recent pass through the solar system was in late 1992. In 1993 Earth passed through a thicker-than-usual part of Swift-Tuttle's debris trail.

For a couple of months in 1993, it looked as if Swift-Tuttle's next trip through the solar system might threaten more than just the space shuttle. Looking ahead, Brian Marsden of the Harvard-Smithsonian Center for Astrophysics calculated that the comet had a one-in-ten-thousand chance of striking Earth

Comet Swift-Tuttle

on August 14, 2126. But Marsden soon revised his estimates. It appears that Swift-Tuttle will be about 15 million miles away when it next crosses Earth's orbit. It's a good thing, too, because the comet measures approximately 6 miles in diameter—about the same size as the cosmic bullet that scientists have linked to the extinction of the dinosaurs. An impacting asteroid 6 miles in diameter packs one billion times as much power as the atomic bomb dropped on Hiroshima, Japan, in 1945.

WATCH THIS SPACE

When will the next big object hit Earth? No one can tell for sure. Only in recent decades have astronomers mounted a serious effort to look for objects on a collision course with Earth. And each year brings previously unseen asteroids out of the dark void of space.

Asteroid 2002 MN is slightly larger than the cosmic bomb that exploded over Tunguska. It passed within 75,000 miles of Earth on June 14, 2002. Astronomers spotted asteroid 2002 MN three days after it had already shot by.

A much larger asteroid passed close to Earth on March 19, 1996. That asteroid, 1996 JA1, measured 0.3 mile in diameter and missed Earth by only 280,000 miles. 1996 JA1 remains the largest-known asteroid to pass that close to Earth.

In March 1998, asteroid 1997 XF11 became the most notorious asteroid in history. Brian Marsden, the astronomer who had predicted that comet Swift-Tuttle might strike Earth in 2126, made a similar prediction for 1997 XF11. This asteroid made instant headlines because, measuring about 1 mile in diameter, it was large enough to cause global destruction.

The University of Arizona's Spacewatch program discovered XF11 on December 7, 1996. In the following months, astronomers in Japan and Texas tracked the asteroid. Based on their observations, Marsden calculated that XF11 might pass within 30,000 miles of Earth on October 26, 2028—and it might even collide with the planet. But two astronomers at NASA's Jet Propulsion Laboratory (JPL) in California quickly announced that, according to their calculations, XF11 would miss Earth by 600,000 miles. At about the same time, XF11 was located in photographs taken by the Palomar Planet-Crossing Asteroid Survey in 1990. The Palomar observations provided additional data supporting the JPL astronomers' claims.

Asteroid 1999 AN10 caused a similar, though less publicized, scare in April 1999. Astronomers originally predicted that AN10, which measured about 1 mile in diameter, had a one-in-one billion chance of colliding with Earth in 2039. These odds are so low, however, that it is more likely that an as yet unknown asteroid will strike Earth.

The XF11 and AN10 predictions fueled a long debate among astronomers about how best to tell the public about such discoveries. Astronomers do not wish to unnecessarily alarm the public over potentially dangerous asteroids that will probably turn out to be completely harmless. Neither, however, do astronomers want to be accused of keeping secrets from the public.

This dilemma led scientists to develop the Torino scale. Richard Binzel of the Massachusetts Institute of Technology designed the scale, which resembles the Richter scale that is used to measure the strength of earthquakes. The Torino scale was named for Torino, Italy, where the scale was officially adopted by the International Astronomical Union in 1999. The scale ranges from 0, meaning that an object is virtually harmless, to 10, indicating that an object is certain to cause a global catastrophe. Asteroid AN10 would initially have registered 1 on the Torino scale. After more information became available, scientists classified this object as 0.

So far, the only asteroid to rate as high as a 2 on the Torino scale is 1950 DA. In April 2002, NASA scientists announced that the odds that 1950 DA would collide with Earth on March 16, 2880, were as high as three hundred to one. Measuring 0.7 mile in diameter, the asteroid was discovered in 1950 by Lick Observatory in California. Additional observations were made by Lowell Observatory in Arizona. These measurements were further enhanced by radar observations taken by NASA's Deep Space Network in Goldstone, California, and the Arecibo Observatory in Puerto Rico.

● THE SKYWATCHERS

One of the largest cosmic bombs that may threaten future generations of earthlings is asteroid Toutatis, which measures about 3 miles in diameter. Toutatis hurtled by Earth at a distance of 2.2 million miles on December 8, 1992. The asteroid will pass only half as far away on September 29, 2004.

NASA carefully watches Toutatis from a tracking station in California's Mohave Desert. Calculations of the asteroid's orbit

NASA's Goldstone Observatory in the Mohave Desert

indicate that Toutatis will present no threat to Earth for at least the next several centuries. After that, who knows?

Within one year of the 1992 Toutatis encounter, the U.S. Congress directed NASA to study the problem and recommend solutions. NASA assembled two study groups. One examined the best ways to search for Earth-threatening asteroids. The other discussed what should be done once a threat appears imminent.

The search group recommended establishing Spaceguard, a network of six 8-foot telescopes located around the world. The network would be devoted to searching for Earth-crossing asteroids (asteroids that pass across Earth's orbit). Each telescope would be equipped with a charge-coupled device, or CCD. CCDs are electronic cameras that allow astronomers to almost instantly identify a fast-moving comet or asteroid against the background of stars.

Without CCDs, the search for near-Earth objects is much more tedious. The old-fashioned way requires the use of a stereoscope—an instrument that allows two images to be viewed at the same time. Astronomers view pairs of images of an area of the sky taken at different times. When they find a point of light in a slightly different position from one image to the next, they have found a comet or asteroid.

In 1998 NASA began the Spaceguard survey in modified form, without the network of 8-foot telescopes, which were determined to be unnecessary. It is expected that the survey will be completed in ten years, rather than in the twenty or twenty-five years that had been estimated in 1992. Spaceguard would have cost an estimated $50 million to establish in 1993, and at least another $10 million each year to maintain. Instead, NASA spends only $3.5 million annually on observations of near-Earth objects.

Spaceguard will enable astronomers to chart most of the largest Earth-crossing asteroids. Asteroids that are smaller, but still dangerous, might still escape detection. So might any number of comets—they take as long as one hundred thousand years to orbit the Sun. We wouldn't be able to see them until the Sun warmed them enough that they began to spout jets of gas and dust. By then they might be only a few months away.

Also in 1998, NASA established a Near-Earth Object Program Office at the Jet Propulsion Laboratory. The office's goal is to locate at least 90 percent of all near-Earth objects that measure at least 0.6 mile in diameter by 2008. There may be over one thousand such objects. About six hundred have been found so far.

In 1932 German astronomer Karl Reinmuth became the first person to discover an Earth-crossing asteroid. The first program devoted to detecting them had to wait until 1973. That year Eugene Shoemaker and Eleanor Helin launched the Palomar Planet-Crossing Asteroid Survey. The survey racked up impressive results, discovering one hundred near-Earth objects and twenty comets. In 1983 Shoemaker began a separate search, the Palomar Asteroid and Comet Survey, with his wife,

Carolyn Shoemaker. It was there that the Shoemakers and David Levy discovered comet Shoemaker-Levy 9 in 1994.

The University of Arizona's Lunar and Planetary Laboratory established its Spacewatch program in 1980. Spacewatch operates two telescopes from Kitt Peak, near Tucson, Arizona. This innovative program was the first to use CCDs to survey the sky for comets and asteroids. It was also the first to detect a near-Earth asteroid by using a CCD. As of July 2001, Spacewatch had discovered 236 near-Earth asteroids and 17 comets. Among its noteworthy discoveries are the smallest known asteroid (one measuring between 13 and 30 feet in diameter) and the closest known approach of an asteroid to Earth (65,100 miles).

The Near Earth Asteroid Tracking (NEAT) system is one of four major U.S.-based cosmic bomb search projects. NEAT began its search for comets and asteroids in December 1995. A joint effort between NASA's Jet Propulsion Laboratory and the U.S. Air Force, NEAT operates two 48-inch telescopes with CCD cameras. One sits high atop Mt. Haleakala on the island of Maui in Hawaii, and the other is at Palomar Observatory, near San Diego, California. NEAT's many discoveries include thirty potentially hazardous asteroids.

As productive as NEAT has been, its discovery power was quickly surpassed by the Massachusetts Institute of Technology's Lincoln Near-Earth Asteroid Research (LINEAR) project, which started in 1996. LINEAR is by far the most productive asteroid search program in the world. Funded by NASA and the U.S. Air Force, LINEAR discovered its first potentially hazardous asteroid in 1997. LINEAR searches for cosmic bombs using a technology originally developed for tracking Earth-orbiting satellites. The program operates two 36-inch telescopes equipped with CCD detectors stationed at the White Sands Missile Range in Socorro, New Mexico.

As of late February 2003, LINEAR had discovered 240 of the 460 known potentially hazardous asteroids. LINEAR's discoveries include asteroid 2002 NT7, which is more than 1 mile wide. For a brief time in July 2002, the month the asteroid was discovered, NASA scientists estimated that NT7 had a 1-in-250,000 chance of colliding with Earth on February 1, 2019. Although the asteroid would cause massive destruction should it hit, its chances of doing so in 2019 are slight.

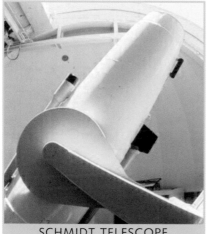
SCHMIDT TELESCOPE

The Lowell Observatory Near-Earth-Object Search (LONEOS) program began operating in 1998. LONEOS sweeps the skies with an automated 24-inch Schmidt telescope and a powerful CCD camera from Anderson Mesa, near Flagstaff, Arizona. By August 2001, LONEOS had already discovered 87 asteroids and 14 comets. Among LONEOS's discoveries is 2001 OG108, which may be the largest known Earth-crossing asteroid. Measuring between 5 and 10 miles in diameter, the asteroid's orbit currently keeps it a safe distance from Earth.

The Panoramic Survey Telescope and Rapid Response System (Pan-STARRS), will get under way in Hawaii in 2006. Pan-STARRS will be operated by the University of Hawaii Institute for Astronomy, with support from the U.S. Air Force. Pan-STARRS, an array of small but technologically sophisticated telescopes, will undertake a variety of astronomical research projects. One of its priorities will be the detection of potentially hazardous asteroids.

Pan-STARRS will be an optical (visible light) survey, as are NEAT, LINEAR, and LONEOS. But astronomers also use radar telescopes to study near-Earth asteroids. In 2000, scientists using the radar telescope at Arecibo Observatory in Puerto Rico discovered the first near-Earth binary asteroid—two asteroids orbiting around one another.

Since then, observations made with NASA's Goldstone, California, tracking telescope facility have shown that about one in every six asteroids larger than 220 yards in diameter is likely to be a binary. This result had been predicted by geological studies of pairs of craters of the same age on Earth and the Moon. Binaries probably form when the gravity of Earth or Mars pulls an asteroid apart during a close encounter. The finding spells double trouble for Earth—there is a significant chance that Earth could be hit by two asteroids at once.

The search for cosmic bombs is an international issue that calls for an international effort. The search is being conducted by both professional and amateur astronomers, not only in the United States, but all around the world. The next step is to figure out the best way to defuse a cosmic bomb once one is found to be on a collision course with Earth.

Chapter 7

DEFENDING PLANET EARTH

Astronomers have proven their skill at finding incoming comets and asteroids. But what to do about objects that threaten Earth is controversial.

Consider the difficulty of protecting an entire planet from an asteroid moving at 45,000 miles an hour, even with many years' warning—worse yet, from a mountain-sized comet traveling at 140,000 miles an hour, with only six months' warning. It is hard enough for NASA to protect space shuttle astronauts in Earth orbit against the threat of a tiny piece of space debris poking along at 20,000 miles an hour. In the weeks following the loss of the space shuttle *Columbia* in February 2003, experts considered space debris one possible cause of *Columbia*'s destruction and the deaths of its brave crew.

One proposal for dealing with an approaching asteroid or comet involves attaching a solar sail to the object. A solar sail is a large, thin sheet of lightweight synthetic material such as Mylar. The Sun emits a steady stream of electromagnetic particles called the solar wind. A solar sail uses these particles for propulsion, the way a sailboat's cloth sail uses wind. Given enough time, the solar wind could gently blow a solar sail–equipped object off its collision course with Earth.

(Left) An artist's interpretation of a space object striking Earth

Nuclear weapons possibly could be used to destroy an asteroid or divert it into a harmless orbit. But many experts are against keeping nuclear bombs for any reason. Others fear that the bombs could be used to cause an impact instead of defend against one. Even if the nuclear weapons are used against asteroids, scientists will have to know what their target is made of before planning the attack.

Stony asteroids and comets are relatively soft. A direct hit on either might simply break them up into many still-dangerous pieces. But detonating a bomb some distance away from the cosmic missile might force it into a new orbit. Iron asteroids, on the other hand, are much harder. Pushing an iron asteroid out of Earth's way would probably require a blast to the surface. In either case, the effects of an explosion would depend partly on whether the asteroid or comet had experienced previous collisions that could have changed its internal structure.

Computer simulations have led some researchers to warn that it would be difficult to predict the effects of a nuclear explosion on an asteroid. The simulations have shown, in fact, that some types of asteroids are virtually impossible to stop or deflect, even with a large explosion.

One University of Arizona scientist has proposed a new alternative to the nuclear defense. He has suggested taking advantage of a phenomenon called the Yarkovsky effect: warmer spots on asteroids give off more heat than cooler areas. Over a long period of time—decades or centuries—such temperature differences have a small but significant effect on an asteroid's orbit. Scientists have used the Yarkovsky effect to help explain how asteroids could have migrated from their original orbits in the asteroid belt between Mars and Jupiter to orbits that bring them near Earth.

Altering the surface temperature of a small but still dangerous asteroid could divert it from a collision course with Earth. This feat could be accomplished by changing the amount of sunlight reflected by the asteroid. Covering part of an asteroid's surface with dirt would cause that area to heat up. Painting a surface white would cool it.

The Yarkovsky method has obvious drawbacks. It will work only on asteroids no larger than 1,000 feet in diameter. Also, its use would require decades of advance warning.

A similar proposal from a NASA scientist involves zapping the asteroid with laser blasts, either from the Moon or from a spacecraft. The resulting explosions on the asteroid's surface would help propel it into a slightly different orbit. A series of such explosions over weeks or months might divert even a large asteroid from its collision course with Earth.

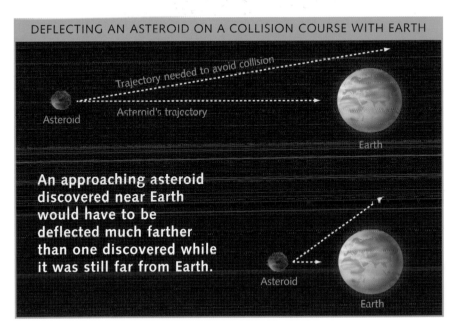

DEFLECTING AN ASTEROID ON A COLLISION COURSE WITH EARTH

Trajectory needed to avoid collision

Asteroid's trajectory

Asteroid

Earth

An approaching asteroid discovered near Earth would have to be deflected much farther than one discovered while it was still far from Earth.

Asteroid

Earth

Regardless of the defense strategy, the easiest objects to protect against would be small ones detected long before they posed a danger to Earth. A large object discovered shortly before impact would be impossible to stop.

● *SHOEMAKER* VISITS AN ASTEROID

Scientists are not just waiting for comets and asteroids to come to Earth. Since Halley's comet returned to Earth's neighborhood in 1986, they have been sending spacecraft to fly by, orbit, and even land on comets and asteroids. The goal of these missions is to better understand planetary formation and the birth of the solar system.

Perhaps the most wildly successful of these missions was NASA's *Near-Earth Asteroid Rendezvous Shoemaker* (*NEAR-Shoemaker*) visit to asteroid Eros. Eros is a near-Earth asteroid—an asteroid whose orbit lies mainly inside the orbit of Mars. *NEAR-Shoemaker* was named for cosmic bomb expert Eugene Shoemaker. Originally scheduled to rendezvous with Eros on January 10, 2000, *NEAR-Shoemaker* experienced technical problems that forced a one-year delay of the historic encounter. But engineers overcame the problems. NASA launched *NEAR-Shoemaker* in February 1996 with six instruments and a bargain-basement price tag of only $118 million.

While en route to Eros, the spacecraft snapped hundreds of photographs of asteroid Mathilde. In passing only 750 miles from Mathilde, *NEAR-Shoemaker* achieved the closest-ever flyby of an asteroid. The *Galileo* spacecraft had made the only two previous asteroid flybys—of Gaspra in 1991 and Ida in 1993—on its way to Jupiter.

The Mathilde flyby provided the first close-up look at a C-type (composed primarily of carbon) asteroid. Scientists prize carbon-rich meteorites as the best-preserved samples available from the birth of the solar system 4.5 billion years ago. *NEAR-Shoemaker* observed that Mathilde had somehow absorbed a significant number of cosmic collisions without completely shattering. Some of Mathilde's craters measured more than 12 miles in diameter. The asteroid itself measures only 38 miles across.

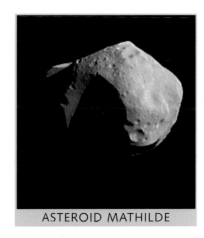

ASTEROID MATHILDE

NEAR-Shoemaker went on to orbit Eros for more than one year. During that time, it produced the first detailed global map of an asteroid.

The craft was designed only to orbit the asteroid. Still, it succeeded in landing on Eros on February 12, 2001. So softly did *NEAR-Shoemaker* land that NASA extended the mission for ten days so the spacecraft could make close-up measurements of the asteroid's surface chemistry.

When the spacecraft landed on Eros in February 2001, the asteroid was 196 million miles from Earth—more than twice the distance from Earth to the Sun. The spacecraft had made a roundabout journey of more than 1 billion miles to get there. The route had been chosen in order to take advantage of a gravitational push from Earth.

Eros is shaped like a potato that measures 21 miles long. It was probably once part of a larger asteroid that shattered in a cosmic collision with yet another asteroid. Eros later suffered more collisions that spotted its surface with craters. The largest

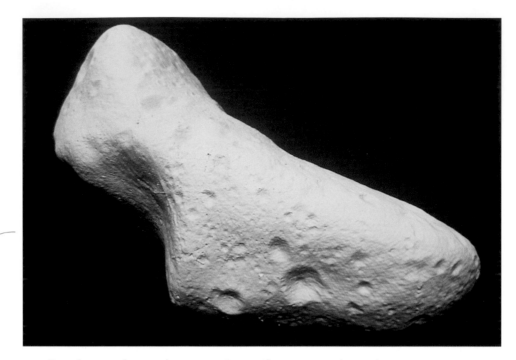

Eros's surface shows craters from many impacts.

of these measures 5 miles in diameter. Even most of the aster-oid's smallest features—dust and fields of small boulders—were caused by impact. The most baffling of the small features were the ponds of dust and small debris at the bottom of Eros's craters. These ponds had settled flat and smooth on the crater bottoms, as if placed there by flowing water. No water has ever flowed on Eros's barren surface, but shaking caused by impacts may have produced similar results.

The *NEAR-Shoemaker* mission was a disappointment in one respect. The spacecraft's enormous stack of data failed to settle a question that scientists had dearly hoped to answer: are most of the meteorites found on Earth fragments of the most common type of asteroid? Eros is an S-type (silicaceous, or stony) asteroid, the most common type. *NEAR-Shoemaker* scientists think it likely that the most common type of meteorites, the ordinary chondrites, come from S-type asteroids, but the data are not absolutely conclusive. Scientists need a sample of an S-type asteroid such as Eros to know for sure. That is because a phenomenon called space weathering changes the surface of asteroids. Space weathering is caused by micrometeorite impacts or the solar wind, or both. Because an asteroid's surface is different from its interior, scientists are uncertain whether instrument readings such as those made by *NEAR-Shoemaker* show what is within the asteroid or only what is at the surface.

Just months after the Eros landing, another NASA mission, *Deep Space 1,* snapped the best pictures ever of a comet. Launched in October 1998, *Deep Space 1* was an engineering mission, designed to test twelve new technologies. After successfully accomplishing that task, the spacecraft flew by asteroid Braille and comet Borrelly.

Like *NEAR-Shoemaker, Deep Space 1* performed a feat for which it was not designed. *Deep Space 1* passed within 2,171 miles of comet Borrelly on September 22, 2001. It did so without special shielding to protect it from the comet's cloud of high-speed dust particles, which potentially could have disabled the craft.

Deep Space 1 got close enough to Borrelly's nucleus to reveal a few details of its complex geology. As expected, the spacecraft's images showed jets of gas and dust spouting from the comet, which resembles a misshapen bowling pin that measures 5 miles long and 2.5 miles wide. Scientists say that the largest of the jets eventually will blast enough material out of the nucleus to cause the comet to break up. The images also

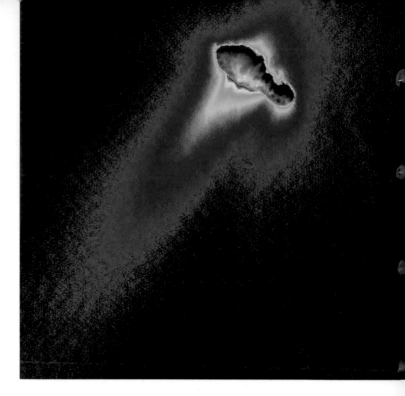

Deep Space 1 took this photo of comet Borrelly. Color has been added to show the jets of gas surrounding the comet's nucleus.

showed rolling hills and plains intermixed with more rugged terrain and deep fractures.

As scientists analyzed the data of the flyby in the following months, they made a surprising discovery: there was no sign of frozen water on the comet's surface. Often called "dirty snowballs," comets contain significant amounts of ice. But a hot, dry crust of sooty material concealed Borrelly's ices.

The *Stardust* spacecraft, launched in February 1999, will fly within 93 miles of the nucleus of comet Wild (pronounced "vihlt") 2 in 2004. *Stardust* is equipped with a special shield to protect the spacecraft against dust particles streaming from the comet. Upon encountering Wild 2, *Stardust* will take the closest-ever pictures of a comet. It will also collect samples of cometary dust, which it will bring back to Earth in 2006. If successful, the mission will be the first to return extraterrestrial material to Earth since *Apollo 17* brought back lunar samples in 1972. The *Stardust* samples will be tiny, but they may reveal whether or not comets delivered the building blocks of life to Earth.

NASA launched yet another comet rendezvous mission in July 2002. Called *Comet Nucleus Tour (CONTOUR)*, the mission was scheduled to encounter comet Encke in November 2003 and comet Schwassman-Wachmann 3 in June 2006. Scientists expected the two comets to provide an unprecedented look at comet diversity. Unfortunately, *CONTOUR*'s controllers lost contact with the probe in August 2002.

The Japan Institute of Space and Astronautical Sciences launched *MUSES-C* in May 2003. It will be the first mission to attempt to bring back samples from an asteroid. *MUSES-C* stands for the third, or C, mission of the *Mu Space Engineering Spacecraft.* The target is asteroid 1998 SF36, which has an estimated diameter of 1,650 feet and will come within 1.3 million miles of Earth in June 2004. *MUSES-C* will arrive at the asteroid in October 2005. It will spend five months mapping SF36's surface, studying its characteristics, and collecting small samples before returning to Earth in June 2007. Scientists have strong suspicions as to what asteroids are made of, but so far they have lacked absolute proof. *MUSES-C* may finally bring astronomers the proof they have been looking for.

BUSY SKIES

Three other missions to comets and asteroids remain to be launched. Comets are the objective for the European Space Agency's ambitious *Rosetta* mission, which will be launched in February 2004, and for NASA's *Deep Impact* mission, scheduled for December 2004. NASA will launch *Dawn,* a mission to orbit the solar system's two largest asteroids, in 2006. This mission aims to provide new information on the birth of the planets.

The *Rosetta* mission was designed to gain new insights into the formation of the solar system. *Rosetta* was originally intended to orbit comet Wirtanen for nearly two years beginning in November 2011. It was to attempt to land a probe on the comet's surface in 2012. The effort, if successful, would have marked the first landing ever made on a comet.

Rosetta's launch was delayed because of the malfunction of an *Ariane 5* rocket in December 2002. This is the same type of rocket that the European Space Agency was planning to use to launch *Rosetta*. Having missed the launch window to reach comet Wirtanen, mission planners have chosen a new comet for *Rosetta* to visit: comet Churyumov-Gerasimenko.

Scientists plan to increase the odds for success by landing their probe on the comet while it is still far from the Sun. At this distance, scientists expect the comet to be relatively inactive. As the comet comes nearer to the Sun, it will begin to emit more jets of gas and dust particles that could prove hazardous to the lander.

Rosetta's instruments will collect data from twenty-one experiments. It will document any changes comet Churyumov-Gerasimenko may undergo as its orbit brings it to within 120 million miles of the Sun.

Deep Impact will be the first mission to examine a comet's interior. The spacecraft will launch an 820-pound copper missile at comet Tempel 1 on July 4, 2005. The missile will blast out a crater as wide as a football field and as deep as a seven-story building. From a distance of 300 miles, *Deep Impact*'s instruments will scan the impact debris and the comet's freshly exposed interior to learn about its structure and composition. The instruments also will record any changes in the gas and dust that the comet emits after the impact. Telescopes on

Earth, meanwhile, will watch as the comet temporarily brightens due to sunlight reflecting off the scattering impact debris.

Although budget problems forced NASA to cancel plans to provide a miniature rover for *MUSES-C,* the U.S. space agency has forged ahead with its own asteroid mission. NASA's *Dawn* spacecraft will begin its nine-year journey to the solar system's two largest asteroids in 2006. *Dawn* will orbit asteroids Vesta and Ceres at distances ranging from 60 to 500 miles, collecting data with a variety of instruments.

Vesta and Ceres, like most other asteroids, inhabit the main asteroid belt between Mars and Jupiter. Ceres, the largest asteroid, measures 580 miles in diameter and may even have a thin atmosphere. Although smaller than Ceres, Vesta, at 320 miles in diameter, is brighter. It is the only asteroid that can be seen from Earth with the naked eye. The two asteroids will provide scientists with a study in contrasts because of their very different histories. Vesta is a dry asteroid that, like the Moon, has extensive lava flows and many impact craters. Ceres, meanwhile, contains water-bearing minerals and has remained largely unchanged since the birth of the solar system.

These missions were largely planned with scientific or engineering goals in mind, not planetary defense from cosmic bombs. Still, the knowledge gained from these space probes will help the experts disarm any future cosmic bomb that may someday threaten Earth.

In the meantime, scientists will continue to hunt for ancient craters back here on Earth. Their discoveries will provide new and ever more detailed insights into the history of killer rocks from outer space.

IMPACT SITES AROUND THE WORLD

Manson

Sudbury

Manicouagan

Charlevoix

Holleford

Haviland

Kentland

Beaverhead

Chesapeake Bay

Meteor Crater
(Barringer)

Chicxulub

This map shows the sites around the world that have been proven to be of impact origin. Sites mentioned in this book are labeled. As scientists identify additional impact structures, they are added to the maps on the Earth Impact Database website, <http://www.unb.ca/passc/ImpactDatabase/>.

GLOSSARY

amino acids: organic molecules, some of which can combine to form proteins

asteroid: a very small planet that travels around the Sun

asteroid belt: the region of space between the orbits of Mars and Jupiter in which most asteroids are found

astroblemes: old craters that have largely disappeared due to erosion and other forces of nature

astronomers: scientists who study the stars, planets, and space

atmosphere: the amount of pressure exerted at sea level by the weight of a column of air extending to the top of Earth's atmosphere

basalt: a kind of mineral formed from solidified lava

buckyball: a spherical molecule made up of sixty carbon atoms bonded to one another; also called buckminsterfullerene or fullerene

catastrophism: the idea that Earth's crust sometimes undergoes quick, massive changes

charge-coupled device (CCD): an electronic camera that allows astronomers to almost instantly identify a fast-moving object against the background of stars

coesite: a mineral formed when quartz is subjected to pressures of more than 30,000 atmospheres

comet: an object with a solid core of ice, dust, and rock that orbits the Sun. As a comet approaches the Sun, the ice in its core turns into gas, creating a long tail that points away from the Sun.

crater: a hole caused by an object hitting the surface of a planet or moon

crosscutting, principle of: the idea that a geologic feature such as an impact scar must be younger than the rock layers it cuts across

Deccan Traps: a vast area of lava flows in west-central India

dinosaur: any of a group of reptile-like animals that lived about 230 million to 65 million years ago. Dinosaurs had an upright posture and spent most or all of their life on land.

Earth-crossing asteroid: an asteroid whose orbit crosses Earth's orbit

fossil: the remains or traces of an animal or plant that lived long ago, preserved as rock

galactic plane: an imaginary plane running through the length and width of the galaxy

geologist: a scientist who studies Earth's crust and the way its layers were formed

impact scar: the eroded remains of an older crater

infrared radiation: radiation that is just beyond red in the spectrum

iridium: an element rare in Earth's crust but common in meteorites

K-T boundary: a distinct, iridium-rich mineral layer deposited between the Cretaceous (K) and Tertiary (T) geologic periods, about sixty-five million years ago

Kuiper belt: a disk of tens of thousands of comets that lies beyond the orbit of Neptune

magma: molten rock found beneath Earth's surface

mantle: the part of Earth's interior that lies below the crust and above the central core

maria (sing. mare): vast, dark areas on the Moon's surface, formed when lava filled large impact basins

mass extinction: a catastrophic event in Earth's history in which large numbers of species died out

meteor: a piece of rock or metal from space that enters Earth's atmosphere at high speed, is made white-hot by friction, and usually burns up completely; a shooting star

meteorite: a mass of metal or stone that has fallen to Earth without vaporizing completely

microtektites: tiny glass pellets produced by impact

Oort cloud: a vast sphere of cometary bodies that encircles the solar system

osmium: a metallic element that is abundant in meteorites but rare in Earth's crust

paleontologist: a scientist who studies fossils

P-T boundary: a distinct mineral layer deposited between the Permian (P) and Triassic (T) geologic periods, about 245 million years ago

quartz: a crystalline mineral

shatter cone: a cone-shaped, wrinkled-looking rock formed under high pressure resulting from meteorite impact

shergottite-nakhlite-chassignite (SNC) meteorites: three types of meteorites that originate from the planet Mars

shocked quartz: quartz that has been damaged by pressures of approximately 10,000 to 20,000 atmospheres

stishovite: a mineral formed when quartz is subjected to pressures of 12,000 to 15,000 atmospheres

strewnfields: areas in which tektites are found

supernova: an exploding star

superposition, principle of: the idea that, except under special circumstances, younger layers of rock always sit atop older layers

tektites: lumps of glass that form when rock is melted by impact and violently ejected from the ground

ultraviolet radiation: radiation that is just beyond violet in the spectrum

uniformitarianism: the theory that processes happening in the present show what happened to Earth's surface in the past

volcanic bombs: blobs of lava that have hardened after being expelled violently into the air

volcanism: volcanic activity

FOR FURTHER READING

Books

Alvarez, Walter. *T. rex and the Crater of Doom*. New York: Vintage Books, 1998.

Bortz, Alfred B. *Martian Fossils on Earth?: The Story of Meteorite ALH 84001*. Brookfield, CT: Millbrook Press, 1997.

Gallant, Roy A. *The Day the Sky Split Apart: Investigating a Cosmic Mystery*. New York: Atheneum, 1995.

Gribbin, John R., and Mary Gribbin. *Fire on Earth: Doomsday, Dinosaurs, and Humankind*. New York: St. Martin's Press, 1996.

Lauber, Patricia. *Voyagers from Space: Meteors and Meteorites*. New York: Crowell, 1989.

Websitcs

1908 Siberia Explosion
<http://www.psi.edu/projects/siberia/siberia.html>
This site is an attempt to reconstruct the 1908 Tunguska impact from eyewitness accounts.

Asteroids: Multimedial Tour
<http://www.geocities.com/zlipanov/main.html>
This site contains information about asteroids, comets, and impact craters, including photos, plus links to the official pages of space missions.

The Barringer Meteorite Crater
<http://www.barringercrater.com>
This is the Barringer Crater Company's site about Meteor Crater. It includes an interactive quiz and a 3-D meteor collision simulation game.

Meteor Crater Enterprises
<http://www.meteorcrater.com/index2.htm>
Meteor Crater Enterprises' website includes a virtual tour of the rim of the crater and an animation of the impact that created the crater.

Zoom Astronomy
<http://www.zoomdinosaurs.com/subjects/astronomy/>
This is the contents page of a comprehensive astronomy site. Topics include asteroids, comets, meteoroids, craters, and the Kuiper belt.

INDEX

ABOUT THE AUTHOR

Steven N. Koppes has spent most of his career as a science writer at major research universities, first at Arizona State University, then at the University of Georgia, and most recently at the University of Chicago. He holds a master's degree in journalism from the University of Kansas. *Killer Rocks from Outer Space* is his first book. He lives in Homewood, Illinois.

For a list of references used in the preparation of this book, see <http://home.comcast.net/~s.koppes/index.html>.

PHOTO ACKNOWLEDGMENTS